IVY AND STEVIE

Ivy & Stevie

Ivy Compton-Burnett and Stevie Smith

CONVERSATIONS
AND REFLECTIONS
BY

Kay Dick

ALLISON & BUSBY
LONDON · NEW YORK

This edition published 1983 by
Allison & Busby Ltd.
6a Noel Street
London W1V 3RB
and distributed in the USA 1983 by
Schocken Books Inc.
200 Madison Avenue
New York, NY 10016

First published 1971
by Gerald Duckworth & Co Ltd.

British Library Cataloguing in Publication Data
Dick, Kay
Ivy and Stevie
I. English literature — 20th century — History and criticism
II. Authors, English — 20th century — Interviews
I. Title
802.9'00914   PR471

ISBN 0-85031-483-6

Printed in Finland by Werner Söderström Oy.

To June and Neville Braybrooke

Illustrations

Contents

Foreword

Since the original publication of *Ivy and Stevie* in 1971, interest in both Ivy Compton-Burnett and Stevie Smith has grown phenomenally, to say the least. Hugh Whitemore's highly acclaimed play, *Stevie* (which is, as the author acknowledges, largely based on material taken from this book), did much to popularize her work for a new readership, as did the film of the play and its subsequent television screening. Following the Collected Edition of her poems (which contains her last poem, "Thoughts about the Stroke", originally printed here), all her novels have been successfully reissued in paperback. Demand for her work inspired *Me Again: the Uncollected Writings* edited by William McBrien and Jack Barbera, who are currently working on a biography.

Similarly, Ivy Compton-Burnett's work has appeared in a Collected Edition from her original publisher, Gollancz, and more recently individual novels have begun to appear in paperback again. Hilary Spurling's long awaited and fascinating second volume of biography will be published next year to coincide with the Ivy Compton-Burnett Centenary.

I feel I must mention that inadvertently and contrary to my intention, biographical information "told me" by Ivy has been taken at face value; in fact, some details of her background came from Ivy's tendency to entertain grandiose fantasies in order to disconcert her listener. In particular, Ivy told me that her family was "raised" on an estate and that as a young man her father had studied under Freud in Vienna (see p. 49). In fact, as Hilary Spurling has shown in her first volume of biography, *Ivy When Young*, Ivy's family moved four times before she was fourteen, "living on housing estates or in brand new suburban developments", and had her father studied under Freud when he was in Vienna (1865), the great man would have been a very precocious nine-year-old.

Thinking about Ivy and Stevie after this interval of twelve years, when at the time of writing I was naturally closer to the grief of Stevie's death, I can now appreciate that the great character link between these two deliberately eccentric artists was their positive delight in a mischievous, although not unkindly, confusion — confusion of us, their admirers. Each, in her own way, was an expert performer, and the role they played to the utmost of their social creativity was being even more themselves than was, at times, necessary. They enjoyed their public personas, and added new bits, as does a comedian. The effect of this was an extension of their individualistic work into their life-style.

Kay Dick
Brighton, 1983

Preface to the First Edition

The origins of this book are only partly fortuitous. For some years now I have been recording conversations with writers and I had planned some day to put the pieces together in a book. When Stevie Smith died earlier this year, not long after Ivy Compton-Burnett, it ocurred to me that public interest in them both was sufficient to warrant publication of these two conversations on their own. As I thought further, it seemed to me that their deaths and my acquaintance were not the only links between them. Both were single, self-reliant women; both were writers of unusual character and originality, who knew each other and admired each other's work; and such differences as there were in their background, way of life and temperament pointed to interesting contrasts between them as individuals and between their different *oeuvres*. Accordingly the two conversations — to which I have added my reflections — are offered here together, in the confidence that neither will detract from the interest of the other and the hope that the contrasts and similarities revealed will have an interest of their own.

Ivy Compton-Burnett

Dame Ivy Compton-Burnett DBE

Born June 5, 1884, at Pinner, Middlesex.

Educated privately, and at Holloway College, where she took a classical degree.

Honorary degree Leeds University and C.B.E. conferred 1951.

Advanced to D.B.E. 1967.

Died August 27, 1969.

Publications: *Dolores*, 1911; *Pastors and Masters*, 1925; *Brothers and Sisters*, 1929; *Men and Wives*, 1931; *More Women Than Men*, 1933; *A House and Its Head*, 1935; *Daughters and Sons*, 1937; *A Family and A Fortune*, 1939; *Parents and Children*, 1941; *Elders and Betters*, 1944; *Manservant and Maidservant*, 1947; *Two Worlds and Their Ways*, 1949; *Darkness and Day*, 1951; *The Present and the Past*, 1953; *Mother and Son* (James Tait Black Memorial Prize), 1955; *A Father and His Fate*, 1957; *A Heritage and Its History*, 1959; *The Mighty and Their Fall*, 1961; *A God and His Gifts*, 1963; *The Last and the First* (posthumously), 1971.

Stage version by Julian Mitchell of *A Heritage and its History*, directed by Frank Hauser, Oxford Playhouse, and The Phoenix Theatre, 1965.

Several novels adapted for broadcasting.

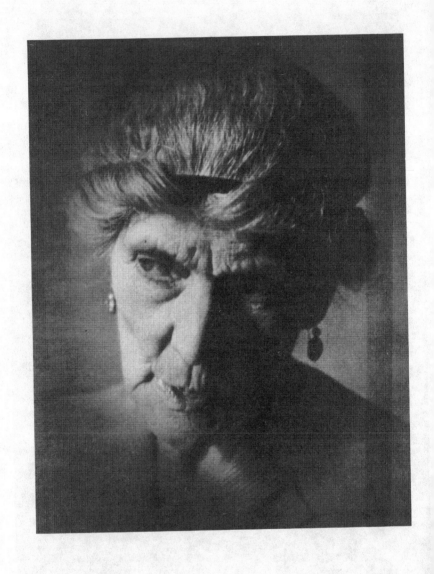

Talking to Ivy

This conversation was recorded on October 9, 1963, between luncheon and tea, at Dame Ivy's Kensington apartment in Cornwall Gardens. Although occasionally she allowed herself to be interviewed (reluctantly, since invariably she was critical of the end product), and was formally recorded by the BBC— once talking about her work to her friend, Miss Margaret Jourdain ('A Conversation', originally published in the first number of *Orion* and later by Nicolson & Watson, 1945) and once in a brief televised interview with Mr. Alan Pryce-Jones*—never had she permitted any off-the-cuff recording of her conversation, such as, I am happy to say, she granted me. My recording was done with the idea that at some future date I would use the material in a written piece. This she knew, and she called our afternoon 'note-taking'. I had no prepared questions, since I had had, before this, much general factual information from her. I placed the microphone near her, and hoped for the best. What is inevitably missing from this printed text is Ivy's constant chorus of 'ums' and 'ers' and her delightful chuckles (the latter when, I suspect, she considered she had got the better of me), and, of course, her inimitable tone of voice—that clear harpsichord harmony, matching the diction of her novels. About six months later she visited me in Hampstead, and insisted on listening to this tape which, clearly, she enjoyed no end. 'We did well', she said. None of it was printed during her lifetime. Three days after she died, some extracts were published in the *Times Saturday Review* (August 30, 1969); and a similar selection appeared in *Harpers Bazaar* in May, 1970. My editing is minimal, mostly confined to cutting my own remarks and references which are of personal and merely private interest.

K.D.: *You once said that Darwin had played a very important part in your life. Possibly you wouldn't say that now?*

I.C.-B. Well, I expect I meant that it was an important

*Then editor of the *Times Literary Supplement*

part in my life when I realized that a man just had a physical ancestor, and wasn't created and all that. Perhaps I meant that, did I?

Yes, because you were talking about your family. You said your family was very High Church.

Well, I went to a High Church school. My family were just Church, and I went to a High Church School, you see, in the next road. I think that was the reason, really. But we had a lot of High Church lessons—history of the prayer book, history of Collects, and all kinds of such things. I think the girls at the school were really confirmed when they were about eleven, but I wasn't, you know.

Were you ever?

Yes, I was, a little later.

And you believed at the time?

I don't think I ever believed in the sense that it meant anything to me. I believed in the sense when I was a child that I thought grown-up people must know, and I just didn't question it. But I never liked the religion. I never liked it.

Any religion?

I wouldn't have said that. I didn't like that religion. I didn't like all the atonement and all that you know. I didn't like it at all. I thought it was a disagreeable and humiliating religion, although I thought it was the right religion, because I didn't question things like that, any more than I questioned that the earth was the shape of an orange. I was just told that. Then, as I grew up, as I got to be sort of 14, 15, 16, as far as one can put it into words, one's reason rejected it. What is your experience?

I'm not quite sure.

Well, that's how it seems to me, and I don't see how people can believe anything.

Of course, your world at that time was so different from what it is now.

Oh yes, very different—very different, but I don't think that human relationships are so different. No, I don't think people are so different. The world was much more self-contained, you know. People didn't go about nearly so much, but I think their human relationships were much the same. Of course, families were larger.

They had such strong beliefs, didn't they? More beliefs than we have?

Some people had the most tremendously strong beliefs.

Wouldn't that have affected their personal relationships?

I think, you know, that a great many people believed as I did when I was a child, but because they hadn't thought to question it.

But you did question—you must have been a born questioner.

Yes. I questioned it because, of course, science came into the air, you see, and Darwin came, and I remember when I was very tiny, about seven, the governess told us that men—I suppose she was modern—descended from monkeys. I remember telling my nurse that she said that, and she said it was very wicked to say that men were not created by the Almighty.

Then you read Darwin yourself?

No, I don't think I read him, or very little, but it was all in the air, you know. It was important in the sense that it put one on the track, but one would have been put on the track anyhow. Of course, I mean science being in the air meant that people questioned things earlier. It seems to me amazing that people should believe these things. This spread of Roman Catholicism—I always do long to ask the converts, 'Do you really accept the dogma?' Don't you? Do you dare to ask them that?

I'm sure you dare anything.

Well, I don't think I have dared. Now, hasn't Alan Pryce-Jones turned Catholic? And Jimmy Lees-Milnes* did, but I believe he's turned back again.

I remember you said that the Catholics were better than the Church of England.

I think they are. I think that Catholic clergymen, Catholic priests—of course, I don't know them, I've never known any—I think that Catholic priests and High Church parsons take a more proper interest in their congregation than Low Church who have rich congregations. I remember our parson in Hove telling my mother he wanted a curate to call on the tradespeople. Well now, I don't think the Catholics are like that. I think every human soul is equal in their sight, and

*Author of architectural and other works.

High Church parsons are much the same. High Anglicans, who are almost Catholics, would be quite in sympathy with Catholicism.

What did your family think?

Oh well, my brothers, the same thing was happening to them as to me.

You came from a very large family didn't you?

Yes, but like all very large families, I lived in one group, you see. I and my two brothers were a group, I think very nearly of an age.

When you say 'group', what do you mean exactly?

I mean three of us apart; the others were older and younger. And in a big family with a big house, there were grown-up people, and there was a schoolroom, and there was a nursery. We were rather self-contained, you know.

What about your father and mother?

Well, my father died when I was only sixteen. My mother, I think, rather lost her beliefs because we did, or sort of half lost them. But she died when she was youngish, too, before she was 56.

Which parent are you like?

I'm supposed to be a cross between them.

And what would you say?

To look at? Oh, I think a little more like my father, two-thirds like my father. But I see the third of my mother in me though.

What was your father like?

He was a big dark man, rather like me in the face, insofar as a big dark man can be like me.

But you're not a big dark woman.

No, no, not at all! But the cut of the face, I mean. The cut of the face is rather like. My mother was fair. I'm a cross between them. She was very fair. Her hair always stayed golden. Several of us started golden, but we went drabber— you know how fair hair so often does. As he died when I was sixteen, and he was in London a great deal, and we weren't in London, I never talked to him about religion, but we used to have family prayers once a week. I remember a thing happening that couldn't possibly happen now. The man-servant used to roar the hymns out in a very loud voice, and the cook—that particular cook we had then was a woman my mother was afraid of, my mother was a woman who feared neither God nor man, but she did fear that cook—and that cook liked singing. She was a Plymouth Brother, and she was always singing hymns, and one of her Temperance hymns was 'I'll drink his water bright'. Well, she used to like these weekly prayers, you see, and she used to love singing, but the manservant drowned her voice, and my mother said, 'Harvey, try to keep your voice back a little, you drown the women's voices.' 'Very good 'um', he said. And my mother said, 'Harvey, don't say very good 'um'. I'm always telling you to say, '*Yes,* very good 'um'. I always remember that scene. Highly impossible in these days, wouldn't it be? To begin with, he wouldn't be there.

You've known so much, haven't you?

Oh yes, I've known quite a different world in a sense—in a sense, but I don't think it's as different as people say. I think that a good many of the differences are aeroplanes and motor cars and things on the top. I don't think that human relationships are very different.

What about views, philosophies, faiths?

Well, I would have thought that people would have lost all their religious beliefs, but apparently they haven't. A lot of them are coming back to them again.

How did your father think? Was he very firm in his beliefs?

Well, all I know is that we had family prayers. He never spoke about it.

What did you feel?

I didn't feel anything at all about it really. I don't think I thought about it in connection with him. I think he believed because everybody did, because, of course, it was a different generation. I think people in those times did, you see. I think people just took it in their stride.

I know you get very annoyed, don't you, when people say that you write about a world that is no longer there, because, as you say, human beings are always there.

Oh, I think the world will always be there. It is true I put my books back, because the kind of world one knows one doesn't know completely until it's finished. In a sense one has to wait until it's finished. Things are so much in a state of flux now. I think that some of these modern books that depict human life with people just roaming about London and living in rooms and sleeping with everybody—it's not interesting, because, of course, I can't read them. Everybody doesn't live like that, do they? People don't all live like Jubb*—they just don't. They live in civilized houses as they always did. They have servants as they always did, although fewer. Supposing I were living fifty years ago, situated as I am, I should have had a house and a cook and a housemaid, and, I suppose, a pony trap and a stable boy, instead of just a flat and one factotum. But that's a superficial difference. I don't think people do alter—if they do, they react back again, don't they? There must be family life.

It's changed, yes. After all it's changed from the family life you've known. We don't have the groups you're talking about.

No, because families are smaller. Though of course they're not in some Catholic families.

Did you get on with the other groups? You said there was one above and one below.

Yes, we got on with them, but we weren't much thrown with them you see. It was rather a different life. Rather like a school.

Did you get to know one another eventually?

Oh, we got to know each other, but much less deeply. My two brothers—one died when he was an undergraduate, of double pneumonia in the holidays, and the other, who was a Fellow of King's at Cambridge, was killed in the Somme battles, when he was only 28.

You always speak so feelingly about the First World War.

How it did come into people's lives! Because all the men were killed. In this war the casualties were much less. Then, in the first war, the officers had to lead their men, and the Germans just knocked the officers off, you see. The second war was differently arranged. Then, everybody with a university degree was given a commission at once, and so had to take the dangerous post. We lost the cream of the generation in the First World War. People like my brother, and Rupert Brooke, and people like that—a generation just went. And they say—I don't vouch for the figures—but they

*Eponymous hero of a novel by Keith Waterhouse.

say that before the first war there were four or five men novelists to one woman, but that in the time between the two wars there were more women. Well, I expect that's because the men were dead, you see, and the women didn't marry so much because there was no one for them to marry, and so they had leisure, and, I think in a good many cases they had money, because their brothers were dead, and all that would tend to writing, wouldn't it, being single, and having some money, and having the time—having no men, you see.

When did you start to write?

I started late.

You wrote one book before the others, didn't you?

Yes, I did that piece of juvenilia [*Dolores*], but my brother meddled with it, and I don't take any interest in it, because I can't remember how much I wrote and how much I didn't really. But people always *will* be prying into it, you know.

And you don't want them to?

I don't remember anything about it. I can't make it up at this stage, and people do like gossip so, don't they?

Of course they do. Don't you, to some extent?

Well no, when I'm reading a writer, I like to read the writer's real books. The ones that the writer would acknowledge as his books. Otherwise I'm not interested in him really.

There were fourteen years between your first and your other books.

Oh, a long time.

You felt like writing, obviously.

Well, I shall have to explain my personal life a bit there. My mother died. I was left at the head of things—for a time, and then the war came, and my brother was killed. I was very knocked about. And then I had a terrible illness—that epidemic of influenza that turned to pneumonia. We didn't have the antibiotics then. One just fought for breath for about a month. Then I got well, but I could do very little for some years, and then as my strength came back my mental strength came back too. But one did get very delayed.

Did you always know you wanted to write?

People always ask me that.

I'm sorry.

People always ask me the same question. I really don't

know. Yes, I think so. I shouldn't have written that piece of juvenilia. We came of a booky family. I think both my brothers and I would have written. I think my brother Guy, the elder one, who died, would have been an historian or something, and the other one, I should think very likely either an historian or a novelist. But he had to work for his Fellowship at King's, you see. He wouldn't have got that until he was 24. And then he began training for the army at 26. So when could he do it? Just disappeared, you see. You've had a smoother generation. Not that it has been all that smooth—it hasn't.

No, nothing is.

But you've had a war.

Not such a war. I do think you're right. The First World War was such a dreadful sentimental thing.

Oh, the First World War was much worse. It was a terrible war, it got into every life, it got into every home. Of course, the bombing wasn't so bad. There was a certain amount. But there wasn't the danger to civilians in the same way. The aeroplanes had developed a lot, you see. We did have bombing, and people were killed and houses were down and all that, but not to the same extent at all.

Then you wrote Pastors and Masters? *How long did it take you to decide to start?*

Oh I don't know at all. I don't know at all. I think it was the instinct one always had and one was getting strong again.

You never fancied an academic career?

I had a classical education at College and all that, and I suppose that's good training. But I never wanted to go on with it. Oh no, I never wanted to be a classical scholar or anything like that. I don't know how I could have been—not a real one.

It's fantastic really what you've done with your work.

It's quite unique, isn't it? Yes, it isn't like anyone else's. One perhaps unconsciously makes a world gradually, by writing always in the same way. Some people write first in one way and then in another. I've always written in the same way, insofar as anyone ever does you know.

But you've produced a particular kind of art, quite different from anyone else's. Yet it has links with the traditional.

Yes, it's traditional in a sense, isn't it. Well, I meant it to be that. Of course, I think one has to work in a world of one's own in a way. Otherwise you'd never get any depth, or anything focused really.

Did you know what you intended to do with your work?

No, I think it just came.

Looking back on it all, there's a tremendous volume now isn't there?

A fair number. Not tremendous. Well yes, because I haven't written any rubbish, you see. So the bulk of it which is reasonably worth reading is larger than some people's who've written much more in bulk. I don't know why I write so much in dialogue. I think it must just have been my nature. It just came like that. I don't think one can explain these things—they probably go deep, these reasons, don't you think?

Yes. Besides you get everything, don't you, in your dialogue, for which other people take pages of descriptive prose?

Oh yes, I do.

You're not concerned, are you, about what people do, so much as with what they think about what they're doing?

Well, people in civilized life don't do much, do they?

People in your books do rather.

Oh yes, they may do real deeds. But I think there are a good many more deeds done than some people know. You've done a deed haven't you?*

Yes. Have you done a deed?

No, I haven't. I haven't been at all deedy. Not at all.

Are you sure you haven't?

Yes, quite sure I haven't. Quite sure I haven't.

That reminds me. You said once you were a woman of blameless character.

So I am.

What do you mean by blameless?

I mean quite perfect morally.

What do you call perfect morally?

Well, I mean without sin.

But what is a sin?

You must recognize certain moral laws. Otherwise you couldn't have any human life, any literature or anything.

*Attempted suicide.

I'd like to know why you think that.

Think what?

What you've just said—that we couldn't have any art or literature without moral laws.

I don't think we could. If we had no moral laws nobody could break them. And no action would have any meaning, any more than if an Alsatian dog kills another dog, just because it's his nature. In a sense all human life must be based on moral laws, mustn't it?

Then we come back to religion. Somebody could say this is faith and belief, but you don't accept that.

Oh no, I think that's something quite different. I think that when people had religion, and thought they would suffer a lot and know everlasting damnation if they sinned, it might have prevented their sinning.

Do you think the intention to sin is as bad as the sin?

Well, morally, I daresay it is.

You think you have committed no sin that you would recognize as such?

No, I don't think so. But then, if people had, I don't think they'd say so necessarily, would they?

Oh, I don't know—one might.

It depends on the sin, of course, and how one saw it.

Of course, it depends on the sin. That's why I'm asking what you'd call a sin.

Give me an example.

Well, adultery, murder.

Yes, I think I should call them sins.

What about vanity?

Oh, I don't call vanity a sin. It's just part of normal human equipment. No, I don't call vanity a sin. It's no more a sin than having a pair of hands.

Self-deception?

Self-deception? I don't think there is such a thing.

Don't you?

No, I don't think there is such a thing as self-deception. When people say they do things unconsciously and sub-consciously, I am quite sure they do them consciously.

You think they jolly well know?

Yes—don't you think they do?

I'm not sure about that.

Well, I think they do.

Mind you, I think they should know.

I think they do know. There may be some people con-stituted so vaguely—though I've never met them—that they don't, but I think on the whole people know.

When people say 'That's my truth for the moment'.

Oh well, their truth may alter, I suppose—from moment to moment.

Some of the characters in your books do that, don't they?

Well, the fact that somebody says, 'That's my truth for the moment' shows it isn't his real truth. Otherwise he'd say, 'This is my truth unto eternity', wouldn't he? If he says it's for the moment, he means what he says.

What about love in your books? People always talk about your method, your manner, but they never seem to me to talk about the love in your books, and yet people do the most desperate deeds for love in your books.

Yes, they do, rather, yes.

Are you conscious of that when you write, that they do these desperate deeds for love?

Well, something has to happen in a book or there would be no book.

Now you're trying to avoid my question.

What is your question? Put it definitely.

You would agree there's nothing really quite definite. It seems to me that in your books love often changes a character's whole way of morality.

Oh well, it does, doesn't it?

You make this very clear.

It puts quite different temptations in people's way.

And they don't come out too well, do they?

Oh no, I don't think they do. People have a way of not coming out well in a temptation. They generally behave quite as ill as they can, don't they? Well, not any worse than I should expect them to behave. I mean, people have to consider themselves before anyone else, don't they, and one wonders what would happen to them if they didn't.

They'd be lost?

Yes, they would, don't you think so?

A sort of self-preservation instinct?

Well, a great deal of it is necessary.

You do put a lot of temptations in your characters' way, don't you? You're conscious of temptation.

I daresay people have temptations: have temptations—one knows they have—and yield to them.

What do you think is the most important thing that makes people themselves in life?

I think a human being is a complex organism. Human beings are not consistent, are they? I think they are consistently what they are. They can be consistently inconsistent. But people are such a mixture of different qualities. You can have such good and bad qualities in the same person.

Do you think creative work is important in people's lives?

Well, yes, I think it is an important thing in the life of the people who do the creative work—or reasonably important.

Would it affect the rest of their lives?

Not necessarily. No, not unless you're the kind of person who writes all day and every day—then it would have to.

Which you're not?

No, no.

Has it affected your life?

I don't think so at all. But then I've always written very spasmodically.

Yet pretty consistently.

I've always broken off if I wanted to. So I don't think it has affected my life. I wrote so late that I can tell. My life went on just the same, really, except that I had the extra occupation.

You have this reputation from your books of being frightfully wise. Do you think you are?

Wise, in what way? Well yes, perhaps one does think one is wise. One thinks one knows, of course. Perhaps that is thinking one is wise?

I was wondering whether you thought it was correct?

But don't you think you know?

Only now and then.

Then perhaps I think I'm wiser than you think you are.

I'm sure you are. By wise one means what? Perception?

Yes, perception, I think, and seeing things as they are,

really, and knowing about things as they are. I think that most intelligent people are wise up to a point in that way.

But you're wise beyond that point, aren't you, sometimes?

I daresay a good many people might feel that about themselves.

Not with reason.

Then without reason.

Supposing I were to ask you some question to which I thought it was important that you should give me the right answer.

Well, I would do my best to. Some people don't. Because I should find any human problem interesting, and give it my whole attention. Some people don't. They give it a very casual attention, and then tell one about an antique they've bought.

Do you get a bit bored with the way they write about your work?

Of course one doesn't always agree—clearly not. On the whole I think I've done rather well. Not so much lately, since the reviewers have been more boyish. I think new fashions have come in rather. I think they'll very likely pass. The very word fashion implies that, doesn't it? I don't think we shall go on for ever having these novels that are pure squalor.

We don't always, do we?

Oh no, there are others. Clearly.

You've had so much commentary on your work, looking at it, thinking about it. Are you happy?

I don't think I think about it much. I feel grateful to the first people who reviewed me when I was rising out of complete obscurity. I think one does. Now, I think all notices are on the whole less good than they used to be. Criticism has deteriorated. The critics talk about themselves too much. So often they have quite a short space, and I always wish they wouldn't waste a quarter of it in talking about themselves so often, which they do.

You've been asked so many times about your titles—they always ask why you choose such extraordinary titles.

Are they extraordinary? They seem to be very normal to me. They always seem to have some relation to the book. So many titles today have no relation to the book at all. They're called something like 'Is it time for luncheon?', and one doesn't know why it's called that.

You've a new book coming?

Yes, it's rather short; it's very short. It's called 'A God and His Gifts'.*

Have you other books in mind?

No, I haven't any book in my mind at all. Absolutely none. I don't know whether anything will come. Perhaps I'm coming to the end. But when I've finished a book I nearly always feel like that for a time—some months.

You once said you thought people had so much creative work in them and that was that.

Well, I think that's probably true. Don't you think so?

I do. I think one must complete oneself.

Yes, I think that's true. Certainly with writers. I don't know whether with painters it would be true of them, because they have their material all before them in a sense, haven't they? We have to dig it out of our insides, don't we?

Do you think that's a harder process?

Well, I believe they say that painters always long to get to their work, writers always hate getting to it. Writers may like it when they get to it, but one always puts off getting to it, doesn't one? They say that painters, because they do things with their hands, are always eager to get back to it.

Why do you think writers find it more difficult to get back to their work?

Well, I think perhaps they haven't the help that having their material, in a way, in front of them, gives them, because, however deeply they go, it must be a sort of starting off for them, mustn't it?

When you start, do you feel this is a digging process?

No, I think I feel on the whole that something's there trying to get out.

Do you think one likes to keep it in?

No, I think one would like to get it out.

But don't you think part of one wants to keep it in too? Once out, it's everyone's isn't it?

Yes, but if you write you mean it to be everyone's.

Do you think one does and one doesn't?

I think when one writes one writes up to a point for readers. I think one feels there's something there and it has to be brought out. It's sort of trying to get out and wants help.

*The last novel published during Dame Ivy's lifetime.

No, I think one wants to have it out.

Because it's a relief, so that something else can be got out afterwards?

Well, it isn't any use if it doesn't come out, is it? People don't really know their own mental processes, and people say, I don't know how true this is, that people work at different levels of consciousness.

I met you first in October.

Was it? When you came to see us* here?

That's right. I'd come from Great Missenden.

That must have been—how many years ago was it? About fifteen? It was not long after the war was it? And you were still in the country. We went once to see you there at the lilac time. More than once. Yes, we did.

It was a very nasty October that year, very cold. You rather doubted whether I could drive home.

I daresay I did. People didn't drive so universally then. Now it seems unusual not to drive. I can't drive. I think that a great thing to be said for London is that people with different incomes live in the same way. Rich people, medium people and poor people—unless you're talking of real poverty —all have the same life in London. In the country they have a very different life.

You're not a Londoner are you, and yet you are.

I've lived in London now, I think, for forty-six years, or forty-seven.

Always the same part?

Yes, more or less the same part.

Didn't you live in Richmond?

Richmond when I was quite a small child. Then we had a house in Hove for a time. We used to go into the country a good deal. No, I wasn't ever settled in London, not in my early days, but it's twenty-nine and a half years since we came to this flat. That's partly why I didn't want to leave it after Margaret died.

Which was the place you liked most?

I think I like living in London best. Because one lives the same as everyone. In the country, with my means, I shouldn't get such a good life.

*The 'us' includes Margaret Jourdain, with whom she lived.

If you had all the means?

Then I don't know. I might like the country life better.

Wouldn't you miss the social life of London?

Yes, I'm a very sociable person. I shouldn't like to change now. I do understand people if they've always lived in the country all their lives and lived, as I say, on very ample means, and I do think a good country life does depend on that, which, in London, it doesn't. You can be what you like in London. It doesn't really matter very much if you have a car and a chauffeur or if you go in a taxi. There's no essential difference.

What about gardens?

A garden is a lovely thing, but there again, it would be a terrible tie if you had no gardener, wouldn't it?

Think of your little London balcony.

I think it's as much as I'd want to do.

You have a very large balcony, haven't you?

Actually I have two balconies, you see. I leave in anything that may come up. I may pot a few bulbs. I very often don't. I always have something going. I grow from seed. If you grow from seed you have to be patient. It's very dull just to buy things in bloom from the florist, isn't it? And expensive too. It's much nicer to know that one has grown them. My long balcony on the north side, you would spend quite a lot if you put nothing in but half-a-crown plants in bloom. I put in little twopenny petunias from Woolworths.

Have you ever thought of writing an autobiography?

No, I think there'd be so much I wouldn't want to reveal. I don't mean important things, but all sorts of hundreds of little things that everybody keeps to himself. I don't think they come into autobiographies at all. Autobiographies would be very much more interesting if they did.

But they did, in the classic ones.

Did they? Tell me one.

Rousseau, Boswell . . .

Yes, so they did. And how much nicer they are because of that. I don't mean things like sex experiences. I mean the sort of things that might sound exceedingly trivial.

To whom?

To the reader.

Does that matter?

Oh no, that doesn't matter. Well, it wouldn't improve the book, would it?

An autobiography would be written from your point of view, wouldn't it?

Yes, I suppose it would. And it won't be written in my case.

Pity!

Well, I think if I wrote an autobiography, a really good one, and put myself into it, I think it would be very interesting, and I think I should do it very well. But I'm not thinking of doing it.

I should adore to read it, and so would you if you were me.

Oh yes, I should. I quite agree.

Do you always know you're going to write another book?

Well, I think I don't so much know, as assume I am. Actually I am a person who could be quite happy without writing.

Are you?

Oh yes, quite sure, because I was. It was when I wasn't strong, certainly. It was when I was delicate and found the day enough without writing. Of course, one can't be quite sure—not as happy, perhaps.

Suppose you hadn't written all these years? You may not have been such a blameless character as you say you are. You might have had to do all sorts of things you didn't like because you weren't writing.

Oh no, I shouldn't have committed crimes because I wasn't writing.

Can you see yourself in life without writing?

I think so, yes. I think I can see most people. Of course, it is a part of it. I suppose it is a different point of view. What about you?

As you know, I'm not working at the moment.

Well, that doesn't count at all. No one is writing the whole time. It makes a thread through one's life. I think everyone wants a thread through his life. In a way some people are happy if they are enthusiastic gardeners or enthusiastic collectors. That makes a thread, I suppose.

One isn't all that keen, in some ways, about writing.

No, because it's more of an effort. I think people enjoy

C

decorating a room and putting furniture into it because their artistic instincts are satisfied without too much effort. Producing something is rather an effort. You may not feel it while you're making it, but you can't go on indefinitely.

Do you feel a great joy when you've finished something?

Not a great joy, no. I feel a sense of satisfaction. That something has been produced. Of course, it's never what one meant it to be.

Have you ever produced something you thought got near it?

I don't think very strongly—perhaps—but I don't mean it very definitely, perhaps *Manservant and Maidservant.* I think that the one I had in my head came out more, because sometimes they do change so. I've found the characters get off. People who don't write say that people who write talk nonsense. Of course characters don't do that, but it does seem as if they do—of course they don't really. One is really doing it unconsciously all the time. But it does feel like that.

You catch your people terribly unawares, don't you?

Oh, I think one has to.

There's a lot of abandon in your people. They don't mind what they say about themselves, do they?

No, they don't. If you're writing in dialogue I think that's necessary. If you cut the dialogue out there's not much left.

Do you find that people you know reveal themselves in their dialogue?

Yes, I think people do. But I think in a book you have to make them reveal more than they would in life. I think everything has to be keyed up more. People are too flat in life to go straight into a book. I think you have to push them to a further degree.

Yet they are, in life, pushed to a further degree, aren't they?

Sometimes they are, at certain moments. And very disconcerting moments they can be.

What question do you most dislike people asking you about your work?

The questions that are asked on the whole again and again—except those questions about that piece of juvenilia*— are generally such simple, superficial questions. They say, 'Do you have a special time for working—so many hours a

**Dolores.*

day? Do you find other people's conversation useful?' I went to a cocktail party the other day, and some woman I was talking to said, 'Musn't this be useful to you?' Of course it wasn't useful. Whatever good would it be to put down, 'Do you feel that draught?', and 'Are you sure you won't have another sandwich?'? Conceit, because they don't say a thing that would be any good at all. One would be only too glad to take it down if one heard something deep or revealing or interesting. Certainly not at a cocktail party, which is a dreadful function in itself. I can't bear them. I went to this one because it was given by the landlord. We're frightfully friendly. That is to say he's frightfully friendly to me. I believe it's because of the enormous rent I pay him. He rather likes my fame, but he thinks of the rent much more.

If you were asking yourself a question, what would you ask?

I should never have to ask myself a question, because I should know. I think people know themselves. I am sure I know myself.

People change. Do you change?

I don't think I have changed much. Of course, the experience one has in a sense one gets to know more, but I don't think one has changed. Insofar as I know people, the sort of essence of them, after they reach about 14 or 15—I put it as early as that—remains the same, more or less. Of course, new experiences alter them in a way, but there's some sort of living core inside them that's always there. Sir Henry Head—the psychologist, you know—said to me once that people could change in a way at any age. As long as there was any energy left at all, there could be changes. It doesn't seem to me, insofar as I've met people and observed them—of course, one has observed them—I think there's a sort of living essence in them that's very different in different people. But there it always is, I think. It's probably decided at the moment of conception.

Someone said there was no evidence so far that there was any innate morality in any of us, that everything had to be learnt.

I think a great deal of morality has to be learnt, and I daresay that the sort of essence in people does get very much modified and influenced by experiences in early childhood and early youth when they're still malleable. But I think there's still something in them that's always there.

What they're going to be they will be?

Yes, I think so. Of course, there'll be surface differences of class and that sort of thing. If you meet people whom you've known a great many years, of course life alters them. They can have troubles, and they can have disappointments or they can be very successful, or they can be very unsuccessful. And life generally seems to bring a bit more bad than good, I think.

Do you think it's people who make it so?

No, I think it's just true. People don't seem to me to alter really. They may come out differently in different circumstances, but I think that they always would have come out in that way in those circumstances, even if the circumstances don't arise.

Does life bring more bad than good?

Well, it seems to, doesn't it? On the whole. One resents misfortune more than one appreciates good fortune. I think one takes good fortune as one's due.

Dreadful things happen to people actually, don't they?
Sometimes.

I don't mean in actual deeds. I mean it's dreadful for them.
Oh sometimes, yes. Oh yes, it's terrible.

Thinking about Ivy

When I first called on Dame Ivy, then Miss Compton-Burnett, in October, 1950, I was a cuckoo in the nest of that select and tenaciously exclusive set of connoisseurs (to describe those dedicated readers of a then relatively minority-cult novelist as fans would be too vulgar a classification, although in fact it was Arnold Bennett who first acclaimed her), because I had not read any of her books. What made this default even more heretical was the purpose of my visit, namely to write a script for the French Service of the BBC relating the woman to her work. My introduction came from Pamela Hansford Johnson, who advised the use of a careless panache to hide my lack of reading.

Ivy welcomed me with grace and some amusement. I felt at ease—this was a trap—because physically she reminded me of a patrician step-aunt I had known in childhood. She was tiny, yet unequivocally imposing. Her physical quality was neat and precise. Her eyes were beautiful, and, most appealing. They reminded me of someone I loved, who had a similar perceptiveness. Her ringed hands were small, delicate, sprightly, and suggested gentleness. She dressed in clothes my mother had once told me were proper attire for elderly ladies—darkish in colour, high-necked, with sensible shoes. She always wore exquisite ear-rings. The ever-debated question of whether or not Ivy wore a wig was settled when, in later years, I visited her in hospital and saw her hair, neatly tressed, hanging down: she wore her hair in that Jane Austen style which her photographs made famous. Later on, I realized that she had lovely legs, because, quite often, she would delve under her skirt for her handkerchief, which she often tucked in her knickers.

We had tea in that large, rather gloomy—yet endearing, when familiar—drawing-room with its high ceiling, Regency mirrors,* solid glass-fronted bookcase, small writing-bureau placed behind the armchair (which no one else, to my know-

*Ivy did not use the fashionable 'looking-glass' term: 'What was good enough for Shakespeare is good enough for me'.

ledge, ever dared sit in), potted plants fronting the three tall
windows mostly blinded over, and its extremely uncomfortable
sofa—on which I perched. It was an austere, near-empty room,
which had its own little corner of comfort and chat within
that cluster of sofa and armchairs facing the fireplace. I
sensed, rather than knew, that there were many beautiful
objects in that room, but I avoided too open a show of
curiosity. 'I am having tea with the famous Miss Compton-
Burnett', I kept telling myself. A new book, *Darkness and
Day*, was due to appear. So enthralled was I with my
experience of tea with Miss Compton-Burnett, that at first I
failed to notice that I was the one who was being questioned.
In fact, with a sparse directness I was soon to recognize as
her forte, Ivy was fast discovering everything about me, and
I was lamentably failing to discover anything about her.

Hampered by not having read any of her books, I stuck to
ambiguous questions about her writing, and was rewarded
rather more than I expected. Our shared distrust of publishers
(a natural compulsion among authors) made her tell me how
badly treated she felt she had been by her earlier ones, and
how she had bought back several dozen copies of her first
book, *Pastors and Masters*. Later, she sold these 126 copies
at a ridiculously low price to an astute Curzon Street book-
seller. After *Brothers and Sisters*, she told me, Heinemann
offered her an advance of £150 for her next novel, which
Sylvia Lynd had recommended Methuen to publish, but they
had offered her only £50 advance. What did she think of her
present publisher, Victor Gollancz? 'He took me out to lunch
once', she said, and that was that.

Why the gap between writing *Dolores* and *Pastors and
Masters?* As in my recorded conversation, Ivy placed the
blame on the war and illness, adding that 'several domestic
upheavals and tragedies' and the death of one of her sisters
had been contributory factors. Then she threw in what I
recognize only now was a bonus, by mentioning the death of
a man for whom she had felt 'great affection' (my memory
suggests that she used the word 'love', but I am not absolutely
certain). 'Surely these are reasons enough?' I felt at the time
there were others which she did not intend to divulge. Finally,
she dismissed *Dolores:* 'It will lead you astray.'

Clearly we were not doing too badly at our first meeting. Then Miss Jourdain—Margaret Jourdain,* with whom Ivy had lived for many years—came into the room. I had been warned about Miss Jourdain's formidable manner and her habit of cutting Ivy's callers down to size. So I was ready for the rap and stood up respectfully. I saw someone whom I can only describe as a cross between the Ladies of Llangollen: a stocky personage, forthright, radiant, wearing white woollen stockings (which were not as fashionable then as they are today), tugging a ring off the third finger of her left hand. She had just come off a train. Another of my mother's dicta came to me: 'Single ladies, when travelling alone in public transport, are advised to wear wedding rings'. Fortunately for me it was one of Miss Jourdain's socially benevolent days, and, contrary to all rumour, this was ever to be my experience, unhappily brief, of Margaret Jourdain.

I felt quite stunned as I sat between the two ladies and was amiably interrogated by both of them—about my reading, not, happily, about Ivy's novels. 'What would you advise us to read?' they innocently asked. I fell right into it, and gave my act of young, up-to-date reader advising two quiet elderly spinsters what titles they should add to their library list. I was being quizzed and had not wit enough to appreciate it until I was outside the flat. Their smiling faces and dutiful nods impressed me—with my own knowledge. Even so, I was given my prize; Ivy was always generous, even in victory. A full drawer of press cuttings and letters was shown me, and I was commanded to make a parcel of them. 'You must come and see us again', they said, I feel certain, in chorus. Away I went, dazed, clutching my parcel, and congratulating myself that the need had not arisen to discuss Miss Compton-Burnett's work. Years later I admitted this to her. She nodded sagely. 'But you have now. You know them very well now, don't you?' Indeed, to make up for my original default, I had read all her books several times. Her tone made it absolutely clear that not only had she known that I had not read any of her books when we first met, but she was hardly surprised that I had not.

*Leading authority on English furniture and author of many works on this subject.

I think that that first meeting set the tone of all our many future meetings. I felt that I was somehow established as one of those near-impossible children in her novels who might do and say anything. She assumed a favourite maiden-aunt quality for me, and, vaguely, I felt adopted. In fact, I suspect, she regarded all my generation as children, and she watched our antics with a sort of measured anticipation. She expected us to behave as we did, and indeed, she was not slow to encourage us in our behaviour.

I loved her dearly. In many areas her views were intransigently reactionary and hopelessly out of touch with life as one knew it. On the other hand, paradoxically, just when one thought her an intolerable bigot, she would lash out with some surprisingly liberal idea, though this was usually in the realm of morality rather than politics. For instance, she fully approved the Wolfenden Report.

I suspect that she took an intense, if partly concealed, pleasure in teasing her conflicting circles of friends and admirers. Her celebrated luncheon and tea parties often consisted of what can only be described as ill-assorted guests, one group of whom would classify the remainder as brainless, boring snobs, who, in their turn, no doubt, regarded them as literary oddities without social assets. In time of course, each faction grew bolder and openly challenged the other's pretensions, which provoked a very lively Ivy indeed, who, expert catalyst that she was, caused all those present to be more outrageously themselves than the occasion merited. It was clearly her favourite game, launching this masters-and-servants or parents-and-children dialogue—the basic pattern of all her novels—with herself presiding, playing the role alternately of hostess and governess.

At first one was invited to tea. And what a tea this was, an old-fashioned nursery tea, with bread and butter, paste, honey, home-made jam, lettuce, radishes, potted shrimps, several kinds of cake and very weak Earl Grey tea. Then one was upgraded to luncheon. Here again the fare was plentiful, plain and good. Ivy much disliked what she called 'messy' food, meaning highly-spiced decorative foreign dishes. Hers was good English household produce. She herself always had an excellent appetite, and urged her guests most insistently to second helpings. Her before-luncheon sherry was, on the whole, unpalatable: one swallowed it down like a dose of medicine, as Ivy watched but did not partake. Her wine was miscellaneous, since much of it came from admirers. She drank her portion much diluted with water. Coffee, served in the drawing-room, was usually accompanied by chocolates or Turkish Delight: she herself had 'a very sweet tooth'. She certainly greatly enjoyed dispensing hospitality. 'Eat up', she would command, 'You look thin', and her tone made one feel that one had not eaten for weeks. She was very keen on punctuality, and once the gong boomed for luncheon or tea, in she marched to the dining-room (a handsome, dimly-lighted, vault-like room) unattended by guests if the guests had failed to arrive on time. Many, myself included, have experienced the maidservant's 'They have started' greeting at the door, and this, literally, within a minute or two's delay.

After Margaret Jourdain's death, in 1951, I progressed to that enviable third stage of Ivy's hospitality, in that after luncheon I was more or less ordered to stay for tea as well, as happened, let me hasten to add, to many others. Ivy admitted to loneliness, quite openly, which was endearing. When one was her only guest a very different atmosphere prevailed; a more relaxed and intensely rewarding communication took place. Then one experienced the Ivy one had grown to love as distinct from the Miss Compton-Burnett image one admired.

Which memory out of twenty years to throw out first? In the beginning, scrupulously, I made notes, and then, probably because I grew so fond of her, I gave this up, simply because Ivy had become part of my life rather than merely the famous novelist I. Compton-Burnett. Our relationship became a matter of fact, not qualified in any way by the disparity in our ages. I am inclined to believe that she grew gentler and kinder as she grew older, but this may merely be that I was myself completely at ease with her.

I was always surprised when someone whom I was taking to meet her admitted to fear, because there was nothing formidable about her. Her manners were quietly gracious, which is not to say that she did not often speak quite sharply about certain people and fashions which she disapproved. To anyone who was inordinately shy Ivy was enormously kind, and took great pains to put him at his ease. Fools, and pretentious ones, she did not suffer. Often she rapped very hard, in her delicate way. 'I won't have their paramours', she would say about certain friends of friends. She rather enjoyed shocking. For instance, she would suddenly interrupt one talking about a mutual acquaintance with a 'Is he an homosexual?' in her best sedate, elderly-lady tone.

She adored gossip, and liked knowing everything about one's private life, which she extracted with great skill; and it was, I suspect, a positive delight to her when she had before her a known gossiper, leading him or her on to divulge the most scandalous details about well-known literary people—gossip which she would later relate, with equal authority, to other gossips.

What particularly interested her was money. How much or how little everyone had whom she knew or did not know— this was proper luncheon or tea conversation. In later years she professed hard times. In fact, often, one actually thought she was really poor, and a remark she made to Kathleen Farrell not long ago typifies this later pose: 'I'm afraid I shall soon have to ask you all to bring your own buns.' Then she laughed. Even so, it came as quite a surprise to many that she left £84,249. This must have been a shock to one well-known novelist who, taken in by Ivy's insistence of increasing poverty, had actually initiated negotiations for benefits to her from The Royal Literary Fund. What Ivy meant, of course, by the threat of impending poverty, was simply the rise in the cost of living. Furthermore, to her way of thinking, capital was not liquid money. She belonged to a generation who simply did not touch capital: to do so was to commit a class-sin. The fact that such basics as rent, rates, electricity, the telephone and food were yearly costing more, spelt poverty. In Ivy's world this meant instability. All this—the threat of imagined poverty—she blamed on the Labour Government—entirely, even when Labour was not in office. It was not so much that she was insular as that she was typically a product of the social environment that had produced her, living still, for all practical purposes, in the era of her childhood and youth. And she tended to regard her visitors as belonging also to that same world. This I think explains her remarks in my recorded conversation relating to the differences between town and country life and to what she called the 'civilized life'. Conversely, she was perfectly able to understand lack of money, and could show real concern, as she did to me, although here again her circumstantial conditioning was such that she added on one occasion, 'Grandmothers never do leave enough do they?' This though I had previously told her that my grandmother had left me nothing whatsoever.

Totally unable to comprehend the existence of social strata below her, or to appreciate that the Welfare State had in fact produced a bloodless revolution which made nonsense of such classifications as 'the lower orders', she clung to her built-in determination to remain where she felt safe—in that solid pre-First World War social order in which certain groups were 'kept in their place'. This was, I feel, a fear of the unknown rather than innate snobbery.

Originally, she told me, her family came from Wiltshire, the village of Compton; she was a descendant of a Bishop Burnett who married a Miss Compton. The family, to use her word, was 'raised' on an estate, and one appreciated the truth of this in her fiction. She adored her father and told me that he was a classical scholar, a great linguist, a doctor trained as a neurologist, and that as a young man he had studied under Freud in Vienna. He married twice; but I cannot remember whether Ivy said that she was the child of the first or of the second wife, this for the simple reason that I cannot now decipher my note on this point. She had a governess until she was fourteen; and then went to a day school, and later to Holloway College. She was born in London, lived in Richmond until she was eight, and then in Hove, and in the country.

I am not writing a biography. That is being done at this moment by two other people, one who knew Ivy well and one who knew her not at all. It will be interesting, not to say highly amusing, to compare these two biographies when they are published, because, judging from rumour, both biographers are being given somewhat different versions of certain facts and incidents by various persons 'in the know'. No doubt within the next few years we shall have a spate of Ivy biographies contradicting these first two. This, I am sure, would have made Ivy chuckle, because she was rather tricky in her confidences, and did not hesitate to supply contradictory versions of the same personal incident to different people. Moreover she often flatly contradicted statements she had made: for instance, I have a definite note, taken immediately after leaving her, that she had read the whole of Darwin, a fact which she repudiates in my recorded conversation. It is in the nature of her fame that we can look forward to some years of biographical confusion, much the same as was experienced by contemporaries of say Byron, Shelley, Carlyle or Wilde (to mention only a few). Eventually, as history proves, art comes into its own and settles the heart of the matter. Moreover, Ivy was slightly wicked, making everyone think that he was her nearest and dearest, and a friend more special than the next. One such proudly told me recently that Ivy had signed all her letters to him 'All my love', which many of us who knew her also had the pleasure of reading at the end of her letters and postcards.

Ivy considered that she had been fortunate to live to be old because she had been given time enough to do her work. If, she said, she had died at forty, the gap of those fourteen years between *Dolores* and *Pastors and Masters* 'would have been a pity'. She wrote in small exercise books—'penny books', she called them. They had to be thin and lined, because her hands were small, and thick notebooks would have been 'uncomfortable' for her to use. She wrote on the right-hand page, using the left for additions and alterations. She did not need 'a constant background' and could write just as well away from home. At one time she told me she did not take notes. Another time she contradicted herself by stating that indeed she did take notes. I have often thought that her habit of talking quietly to herself while one was answering her was a form of mental note-taking. Perhaps she was re-translating into her inimitable prose some of one's sillier utterances. This habit, initially disconcerting, one grew fond of, and indeed waited for.

She once made the fascinating observation that her mother was irritated by the separation of men and women in church: Ivy herself thought that perhaps 'the immediate presence of women would distract the men', and that her mother, 'unable to believe that the sight of her ankles could excite her sons', did not like this practice of the family having to sit apart. Often she was made to feel guilty by her nurse, the 'under-nurse' who looked after her, who always said, when it thundered, 'That is God, angry with you', because she, Ivy, had hit one of her brothers or stolen a chocolate.

She liked a cool bedroom and a warm bed, preferably linen sheets, and a warm room for dressing in. She did not fret about household arrangements. In her younger days she had rather liked painting woodwork; in fact, in her time, she had become so enthusiastic with the brush that often she painted things that did not need painting at all. She said proudly that if she undertook any household task she did it efficiently and with the minimum of time and trouble. For instance, she would buy a piece of satin and make two cushion covers in 'an hour or so'. What she did in this sphere she performed with speed, and what she could not do she would not attempt. People today 'fuss too much', she felt. When she was young she always lived in houses with cracks everywhere, and no one bothered about them: the cracks became bigger but the houses did not fall down. She considered close-carpeted floors 'not quite clean,' and preferred wood-block flooring. She herself liked her main meal of the day in the evening, unless she had friends to luncheon; then she would have 'a little tray' in the drawing-room, with some cheese, salad and fruit. Often, during the night, she would go into the kitchen, 'and eat whatever is there'—sweet biscuits, or a glass of milk, occasionally making herself some bread and milk. She suffered from insomnia but said that, apart from her excursions into the kitchen, she did not give in to it. She would read and lie dozing. Before her accident (when she fell and broke her hip), she enjoyed doing her own shopping. She loved pottering about her balcony garden and was proud of her flourishing plants: 'I let them have their heads'.

One day, for some totally unexplained reason, she suddenly gave me a small photograph of a young woman wearing a very big hat. 'We lived together before I lived with Margaret', she said. 'She married.' 'Thank you', I said, too astonished to ask anything further.

When Ivy died we were shocked, as though the unexpected had happened, though she had been getting frailer and frailer, largely as a result of her two unfortunate accidents. First she had fallen and broken a hip. Then, having bravely endured a year's learning to manage with a frame, she fell again and broke the other hip. I say 'shocked' because somehow she seemed almost an indestructible part of one's life. Among those who knew her there was always that 'Have you seen Ivy recently?' greeting, a chain one took for granted. Also, mentally, although towards the end her memory suffered some lack of cohesion, she remained extremely alert intellectually, reading almost every book mentioned by her many visitors. She was always deeply concerned with a writer's life and its attendant problems. Her probings about this brought out her most genuine sympathy. It was not an easy task this 'extra occupation' she herself had taken on, and she was, I think, most happy about the appeal her work had for younger readers.

Her death was expected, if only because of her great age; yet when the news came there was incredulous grief. Part of one's own life seemed to have been chipped off—though this, of course, is a truism about the death of anyone known and loved. The funeral was an incredibly macabre event, starting with the cremation service at Putney Vale cemetery. There was something unreal, in the Jamesian sense, about the various groupings of family and friends, as people hovered about uneasily, like uncertain ghosts, before shuffling into the chapel. The scene was archaic in an offbeat way. It was as though we were all part of some lightly coloured Victorian print, in varying shades of green, with pale sunlight. Voices were heard. Fluted whispers identified certain people, speculating about others. Those who knew one another rushed together, and then broke away, to stand immobile, watching, waiting— for what? Did we expect Ivy herself to appear? I almost did.

There was one elegantly clothed young man who attracted attention by some romantic aura he possessed, and caught many an eye, and all eyes that day were roving. And there were Ivy's sisters. We looked, but did not quite manage to isolate them visually. We were told that we were expected to foregather at Ivy's Kensington flat after the service. The service? Well, possibly the least said the better about that pedantic, cliche-ridden, platitudinously-mouthed verbiage addressed to the small coffin that was to be lowered so soon into the crematorium ovens. It was, to put it mildly, a ridiculous travesty of what Ivy herself believed in, or rather a travesty of what Ivy did not believe in.

By one of those remarkable yet ever-occurring coincidences, we all went through the front-door of Ivy's flat at four sharp— but no gong boomed. Tea (weak as ever) and sherry (indifferent as ever) were served. I believe I held a cup of tea in one hand and a glass of sherry in the other, as did several other people. We were told that we were each to take away, that very day, after the tea and sherry, the article that Ivy had bequeathed to us, signing for it in front of Ivy's solicitor. It was an order. In her will, Ivy had listed every item very precisely. To her publishers she left a large sum to finance a special edition of her works (excluding *Dolores*). And to six of her closest and oldest friends she left £10,000 each. Apart from Robert Liddell (who has perhaps written better than anyone about Ivy's work and who, in my opinion, should have been nominated as her official biographer), all the main beneficiaries, I believe, were present that afternoon There was, I suspect, some rivalry afoot, because one of them (for no known reason) donned Ivy's maidservant's apron and went about flicking with a duster at the furniture—much of which was fast disappearing as legatees came into their own. Possibly this unique expression was establishing precedence over the others.

The cemetery mood of Jamesian mystery suddenly erupted into one of Ivy's novels. One could readily imagine that she had actually written the dialogue, as voices (non-fluted now) bubbled out 'my favourite Ivy story'. It might have been a cocktail party, that function which Ivy most disliked. Everyone peered at everyone else's bequest, and many were heard to complain that theirs was of lesser account than someone else's.

The young man whose romantic aspect had caught my eye at Putney Vale came towards me and introduced himself. Before he spoke, I felt I had seen his face before. He told me his name: he was the son of the woman whose photograph Ivy had, for some unexplained reason, given me years before.

As people left Ivy's flat, lugging their loot down the stairs, I was reminded of the death scene in *Zorba the Greek*. I believe it was Julian Mitchell who wryly said, as he passed me on the stairs, that he felt 'like a criminal'. Indeed, this staggering finale was reducing us all to that level. Possibly the most bizarre touch of all, which really did convince me that Ivy had written the script, was the maidservant standing at the door, thanking each departing guest for coming and asking everyone to come again to tea. This upset some people; they viewed it as disrespect. I found it quite proper and in its place, and assured the maidservant (who was after all merely repeating a formality of Ivy's training) that indeed I would be happy to come again, knowing, of course, that, unhappily, never again would I be invited to tea by Ivy.

Stevie Smith

Stevie Smith

Born Florence Margaret, September 20, 1902, at Hull. Educated at Palmers Green High School and the North London Collegiate School for Girls.

Awarded the Cholmondeley Award for Poetry, and, in 1969, the Queen's Gold Medal for Poetry.

Died March 7, 1971.

Publications: Prose: *Novel on Yellow Paper*, 1936; *Over the Frontier*, 1938; *The Holiday*, 1949; Poetry and Drawings: *A Good Time Was Had By All*, 1937; *Tender Only To One*, 1938; *Mother What Is Man?* 1942;, *Harold's Leap*, 1950; *Not Waving But Drowning*, 1957; *Some Are More Human Than Others*, 1956; *Selected Poems*, 1962; *The Frog Prince and Other Poems*, 1966; *The Best Beast*, 1969 (USA) *Collected Poems*, 1975; *Me Again: The Uncollected Writings*, 1981

Talking to Stevie

This conversation was recorded on November 7, 1970, during an afternoon and early evening visit, in the front parlour of Stevie Smith's Palmers Green Victorian villa, where she lived for 64 of her 68 years. It was arranged that I be there at 2.30; but, because of good train connections, I arrived a few minutes after two o'clock. I rang the bell, which had a very loud clang, and waited. Nothing happened. I knocked on the glass-fronted door. Again nothing. I peered through the letter-box: the hall looked as though no one had passed through it for months. I pressed my face to the front-room window: no sign of life was to be seen through the lace curtains. I shouted 'Stevie' to the silent house, looking up at the front bedroom: no curtain flickered. It was raining.

A fortnight before, I had fixed our tape-recording session only to receive no answer when I telephoned in the morning of the appointed day. Some instinct saved me from making a fruitless journey, because, when I rang the next day, Stevie told me that she had gone out because I had not telephoned the night before. This time I did telephone the night before. Perhaps she had gone out to lunch and was late returning, or had popped round to a local shop for some cakes or cigarettes? For twenty-eight minutes I made little sorties from under the porch (it was raining very hard now), inspecting the pleasant unbusy suburban street of similar semi-detached houses, keeping Stevie's well-kept trim red-brick-with-white-facing house well in sight, her hedge shaped like a dozing lioness, her patchy plot of front lawn. At 2.30 sharp I rang and knocked yet again. The door opened immediately. There stood Stevie, yawning. 'Oh, hallo Kay', she said. 'Have you been waiting?' We dispensed with explanations: slightly damp, I went in.

I had been in the house before, several times, when Stevie's aunt was alive—she died in 1968. Little change was evident: still the same cluttered atmosphere almost from another era;

accumulated family possessions and bric-a-brac: little was ever thrown away. Shabby furniture, paintings on the walls (mostly executed by Stevie's mother and aunt), books everywhere (an unused piano was piled high with them), a front parlour, a back parlour, a primitive kitchen with a back door leading to an informal garden, three bedrooms upstairs, a bathroom. By no means a dark house. A small family house without a family and yet stuffed with life.

I had known Stevie for twenty-eight years. She knew I wanted material which she had not given to anyone else, insofar as this kind of exclusiveness is possible. Like Ivy she had not much good to say about formal newspaper interviews, and approved only of two short ones—one by Giles Gordon in the *Scotsman* (April 24, 1965), the other by a poet she much admired, John Horder, in the *Guardian* (June 7, 1965). She was impressed by the length of my tape. 'It's very flattering', she said. We agreed to talk off the cuff, and let the tape run on until it was finished—and indeed it finished, oddly enough, on a last word in one of Stevie's paragraphs. We had tea twice, inspected the house, and looked through a load of Stevie's drawings, which she kept in a big old-fashioned playbox along with her income tax and investment papers.

My editing is restricted to reducing my own remarks to a necessary minimum and to deleting slightly indiscreet comments about mutual friends, Stevie's stories about people I did not know, and some irrelevant, though amusing, details about her readings at various schools (Westminster, Eton, and so on) and her public appearances at the Aldeburgh and Edinburgh festivals. Oddly enough we spoke about Ivy, whose hospitality Stevie found 'very odd'; unfortunately this comment was not extended, and Stevie went on to talk about the friend who had introduced her to Ivy.

Stevie was at her liveliest, full of laughter. Like Ivy she was given to chuckling, but hers had a more drawn-out and rollicking sound. She looked remarkably youthful (I was amazed when I read her age in the obituary notices): physically frail certainly—this because of her tiny stature—and yet packed with nervous energy, which was almost a physical attribute, and full of affection and gaiety. At parting she gave me a small stone carving of a seal pup, one of three animal carvings sent her by an Eskimo fan.

I little appreciated at the time how so much of our recorded conversation would soon acquire tragic undertones, because a week later she wrote to me from Devon, where she had gone to look after her sister who had had a stroke, that she was beginning to have dizzy fits and would not be able to travel again for some time. Shortly after this came the news that she was in hospital in Devon, with an inoperable brain tumour. She died, almost serenely one was told, on Sunday, March 7, 1971.

S.S. Yesterday I had to go and record this 'Dial A Poem' in this 'Poet of the Week' thing the Post Office is running and the telephone broke down. I managed to get three poems into two-and-a-half minutes which is quite a record. Anyone who dials this number—it's in *The Times*, dear—for one whole week, can hear the poem. Well, because I broke down, or the machine did, they're keeping me on for another week. The engineer was very superior towards these inferior beings like poets and artists, but in the end he was extraordinarily nice and we had a good giggle. They started with Day Lewis, then Roy Fuller, then me, and after me Dannie Abse. I was paid ten pounds. I gave them my 'Old Sweet Dove of Wiveton' which I do adore so because my Norfolk holidays come into it, 'Tenurious and Precarious' and a little short one about Lucretia Borgia. Rather fun, I rather enjoyed doing it.

(*When questioned about her age, date of birth, she was reluctant to give this and when asked why said*):

Well, I think it's a sort of gimmick, I mean it's such a journalistic thing, and it's very much a British journalistic thing. It isn't awfully significant, as long as you roughly know what decade—say the sixties.

(*We talked about the time we spent together at Newnes, when I was Assistant Editor of* John O'London's *and she was secretary to Neville Pearson.*)

D'you know, I don't remember a thing about *John O'London's*, and that is very odd because I was there for a very long time. I must have been at Newnes for about thirty years, and yet when I left it sort of wiped off. It must have been an awful strain. It was an awful strain. I got really frightfully ill and I had to leave because of illness. I always said to my unfortunate employer, 'Well, I'm not really here.' Now this is a very profound remark to make because the accent's on the 'really'. You see, I must have felt all the time, 'My real me is not really here.' It's a very neurotic thing because actually of course my real me was. I got frightfully tired. I didn't want to be there. As I couldn't actually escape I pretended I had escaped. It was a toss-up. I didn't want the sort of job where I had to use up my whole energy, as I should have done on the editorial side, because I don't have an awful lot of energy. I really am awfully undersupplied with energy.

(She then said this showed in her photographs which was why she hated being photographed. I asked why she hated this.)

I don't like it because of the results. They make me look dead, and as if I'd been dead for a long time. What I object to about my photographs is that I look so ill in them, and I don't think I actually do look ill. I haven't got a thing about age, but I do rather have a thing about looking dead and buried.

K.D. *Were you born here?*

I was born in Hull. I came south at three—south of Hull that is. I had my fourth birthday just after we arrived here. Yes, just as I couldn't think of another job, I couldn't think of another house after Aunt died. As a baby I almost died. My sister and I, we didn't make a very good first appearance in the world. My grandfather was a chief engineer—consultant engineer—one of six appointed as honorary chief engineers to advise their Lordships at the Admiralty, and their Lordships of course were furious and never called them in on any problem—they thought the Navy could solve anything without calling in civil engineers. Grandfather had a gold uniform which he was very proud of. Daddy was in the North Sea Patrol. I didn't like him very much. As you know, I've written so much about the poor man in *Novel on Yellow Paper*. As a matter of fact I didn't like him. He ran away to sea. He wanted to go into the Navy. It was arranged that he go into the Navy straight from school, and then his two elder brothers were drowned, and his mother said no son of hers would go to sea, so he went into the business—a sort of shipping business. Well, I mean, it just went to rack and ruin, and then was sold for a song—all those wonderful clichés come in—'rack and ruin', and 'sold for a song'. I think 'rack and ruin' and 'sold for a song' would make two poems. This was just after I'd been born, and poor Daddy took one look at me and rushed away to sea. Of course, the result was we had very little money, and then my poor mamma, who was ill herself, came to London. Oh, they worked it out very carefully, these two sheltered ladies; her sister came too, my darling Aunt.

Was your mother beautiful?

Yes, I think she was, and so was my aunt. Father was quite good-looking—darkish. The things I didn't like about him were that he would always twist everything round so that it was always somebody else's fault and not his, and in the end he'd practically get people to apologize for something that he'd done which was incredibly stupid. He was a tremendous old egotist. Not happily married—he wanted a career at sea. When I grew up I realized it was what's called an unsuitable marriage, but he used to come home on leave. My mother was immensely loyal; no word was ever said against this creature, and appearances were kept up, and he was very sentimental, the poor old thing, Daddy was, so we'd have to come down from bed, and I had to sit on his knee, you know, and be affectionate to the poor old darling, and I used to think, 'Twenty-four hours' leave. I think I can stand it. It's expected of one. It's the least I can do, there's poor Daddy up in the snow and ice off Iceland.' He was on this Northern patrol an awful lot of the time, a very nasty patrol; he loved the sun and the sea and he would have loved the south. He once got sent off to a southern patrol and we sent his white clothes after him, but as soon as they got to him, he had to come back, to the Baltic. I couldn't myself have been very fond of a man like that, because fundamentally he was a bore, as all very egotistical, selfish people are bores. I thought he was the most fearful bore. I didn't know when I was a child what it was I didn't like, but I suppose I just didn't like that. After mother's death he married again, an awfully nice woman who lived in the country, and who used to call him Tootles, so she must have loved him. I thought to myself, 'Well, if he can inspire someone to call him Tootles, there must be things about him that I don't see.'

What about your mother?

Mother died when I was sixteen. They were two sisters as Molly and I are. Oh, they were so sweet. They were so tremendously sort of loyal and brave, I think. No money you know, and to bring up these two children—two very ill children too—of course I was a fearful handicap, almost a dead loss. I mean, when I was five I had to go away to hospital for three years—a thing they now cure in six weeks, tuberculosis. My mother's family were all dead. Mother had money she'd inherited from grandpa, and on that money they lived, but though it should have been quite a lot in those days it was wrongly invested, and nobody to look after it, and they were so innocent, these ladies. Terribly sad really, and both so sweet.

They painted a lot, I believe?

Yes, these paintings are theirs. My aunt never touched a paintbrush after she left school, but my mother did. Then those holidays. I don't know how they managed because really there wasn't much money, but always there was somehow enough money produced to go for long holidays on the East Coast which I adored, places like Saltfleet where we used to dig for bones—animals' bones in the sandhills. I remember getting a dog's jawbone with all the teeth in it, and I was terribly thrilled about it. I insisted on bringing it home. You'll find all this in my poem 'House of Female Habitation', it's absolutely autobiographical. That's why I feel I'm not betraying all sorts of secrets: mother and aunt were extremely discreet. My 'House of Mercy' poem is this house, here in Palmers Green, although I made the drawing obviously country, and this is a little terrace house. When I came here it was open country. This was just a little terrace of houses—enormously cheap they were then—and all the rest fields.

What did your aunt think of your work?

Oh, her attitude was simply splendid, everything one asks for really. I should hate to live with a literary aunt. My aunt used to say, 'I'm very glad to hear you've got another book coming out, but as you know I don't know much about it.

It's all nonsense to me, my dear.' I felt this was the right attitude. My aunt had a faintly sardonic attitude, I think, to the whole world. Her highest praise was when, after I got the Cholmondeley Award, she said, 'I wish your mother was alive and could have known about this dear.' This would be her highest praise. She was tremendously sensitive and a very reserved woman. I remember when they were going to make a film of me, for *Monitor*, Jonathan Miller wanted to come out here, and my aunt said, 'Come out here? I can't possibly have these men out here.' So I said to Jonathan, 'It would upset my aunt, and she's an old lady. I simply won't have it. You'll just have to find somewhere else.' So they must have got into a slight muddle, because they chose a house at Parsons Green, which is far west of London, near Putney. So I said, 'Well, it's rather a long way isn't it?' 'Oh, we'll send a taxi for you', they said. 'Well', I said. 'It's easier to get there by train, because taxis are never heated in the morning.' The taxi arrived—it was in January—and by the time we got to Parsons Green I was practically frozen. Then we went in; a house slightly like this, larger; it was immediately opposite a school, so we had to keep knocking off, waiting for the children to finish their playtime and go in again, because the noise was so terrific that we couldn't do a thing, and this went on and on, and then, if it wasn't that, the aeroplanes would be coming in. It was all right in the end as these things often are, but the worse catastrophe was when the old lady down in the basement—the housekeeper— thought she'd get on with her ironing, and of course every light in the place fused. I haven't got television. I went round to the vicar's to see it. There was dead silence after- wards. The vicar said, 'You do look so terribly ill, Stevie.' Everybody who sees me in a film says the same thing. I don't think there's much difference between looking ill and looking old. One doesn't really bother about it. But when people come up to one in the street and say, 'You look so much better than you did in the film', you think they've got a permanent picture of you groaning for burial.

When's your birthday?

My birthday's on September 20. I'm a Virgo although I think I'm a bit of Libra too. I've come to the conclusion that

all those people who do the stars don't like Virgo. They think
Virgo's an old-fashioned prim old schoolmistress. Of course
they always give them the worst characteristics. They say,
'Always worrying about detail', a thing I never worry about;
'very good at mathematics'—well, I'm bad at mathematics.

Since you've retired, how do you feel?

I really enjoy life so much since I've retired. When I left
the office, life was absolutely marvellous. I'm terribly pro old
age really, because it's so relaxed, you know, oh so marvellous.
You just go around and do exactly what you like, and somehow it's so delightful. If you want to write you write, and if
you don't you don't have to. Mind you, it means you've
got to have some money behind you. It wouldn't be fun
without any money. You don't need an awful lot—just a
little money. I can't drive a car. Therefore it's no temptation
for me to have a car. I don't like expensive holidays. I don't
want to go abroad ever. I have been abroad a lot. I don't
mind going abroad if I'm going with friends. I was awfully
nervous when I was in Germany just before the war. That
was '31. I was the first of the last trains from Berlin. You
know that stream of last trains from Berlin about '39. Well,
I was positively the first last train. I always feel when I'm
abroad that I know it so well. I suppose I've been to all the
wrong places. I've been to Potsdam, Amsterdam, Königsberg,
and other places where nobody else seems to go. Sort of
student exchange holidays. Then for three long weeks, and
long weeks they were, I stayed at Milan. I always stay with
people who live there, and who are so bored they won't
go anywhere, and they're generally quarrelling with each
other as well. The very opposite of a tourist's holiday. I
think I'm just about ripe now for a tourist's holiday.

Why were you called Stevie?

That was long before I started writing, when I was 19 or
20. I'm christened Florence Margaret, but I was always called
Peggy—Paggy, with a faint Yorkshire accent—by my aunt.
When I was going to take over and the poor darling had to
live upstairs because she couldn't manage, she'd say, 'I don't
know what Paggy will do.' I hadn't been allowed in the
kitchen. I couldn't boil an egg. I got to do it very quickly
because I like food you see. I like cooking. Aunt wouldn't let

me cook when she was in charge. 'This is my province', she'd say. 'What will Paggy do? Paggy will have no one to turn to'—this was so sweet. Well, to go back to why I'm called Stevie. I remember this awfully well. It was a very hot day and I was riding with this man who was a friend of ours—Tooting Bec or one of the London commons—and I was riding on a sort of dull horse you get, one of those hires, poor old thing. It wasn't fed properly; it wouldn't move, so I stood up and kicked it, I'm afraid—not very hard. I was riding in a shirt, which annoyed Arnold very much. He thought it was most improper. And then all the little boys shouted 'Come on Steve!' He was the favourite jockey at the time, Steve Donaghue. So Arnold said, 'It suits you very well, you look like a jockey, you ride like a jockey, I shall call you Steve.' Then it got to Stevie. Now this was given like that, then it stuck permanently.

What did your aunt think?

I don't think she minded. It was beneath her notice. She always called me Peggy, or rather Paggy.

How do you feel living alone now?

It's rather odd really now, living in this house absolutely alone, after having more people here. I miss aunt awfully. I like it now. I would hate to have anyone here. It's wonderfully dreamy to be in a house to oneself. One can wander round from room to room. You can sleep in a different room every night if you want. It's wonderful. I'd hate to have anyone living in the house. You pay the price in a way, that at times it's too lonely. But it's better to be too lonely than too much with people you don't like. The worse thing in life is to be at close company with people you don't like very much. You'd soon get to hate them, and I see nothing ahead but murder or suicide, which ever gets in first. I wish there were a balance, but the fact is I'm too lazy to go into London. All my friends live in London—well, most of them. I only know one person out here. The people I knew are dead, or away, or married. Then I was away a lot when I went to school, the North London Collegiate. I had to go and read at my school, fifty years exactly after leaving. They were very sweet. The headmistress was charming, which headmistresses were not always to me. I often read at schools.

You like reading your own poems?

If you hear somebody else read them you realize how terribly wrong they can get. They actually get the wrong meaning. There's a certain amount of syncopation in them too which you must get right, or it puts the line out. Yes, I do like doing it now. The audience suddenly comes to life. I was not asked to read at the International Poetry reading organized by Spender and Auden. An awfully nice young man wrote to me and said, 'We do so want you to read.' I said, 'Why don't you ask me?' 'But we must have English poets who live abroad.' 'Well', I said, 'I don't mind going abroad for a fortnight'—like putting up the banns. I like singing my poems very much. I haven't any sense of pitch. It must be very painful. Actually, when I was at the North London Collegiate I was asked not to sing, politely, because I put the other little girls off.

Are you going to write any more prose works?

I don't think so. I don't feel I want to. I do think one wants much more energy, because with a poem you can carry it round while you're doing the housework. If you wake up at night you can think about it, and I think about it all the time in bed. It doesn't take too much energy, which actually novel writing does. Then you can't have too many interruptions.

What about your drawings?

Oh, I've got a boxful of drawings. Would you like to know where I keep my drawings? I'll show you. This is a playbox. I keep them here with my income tax and investments on top of the drawings. I had a lot of stocks and shares, because I had this mad sort of foreigner who did all my investments. He absolutely doubled everything. Alas, he got huffy—he was very temperamental. The drawings don't really have anything to do with the poems. If you go through them you can generally find something that hasn't been used before. I can't paint but I think I could colour sketches. That would be very attractive, I think. I think I'll colour sketches now. There's a terrible lot of fear of life in my poems. I love life. I adore it, but only because I keep myself well on the edge. I wouldn't commit myself to anything. I can always get out if I want to. I think this is a terribly cowardly attitude to

life. I'm very ashamed of it, but there it is, dear. I love death,
I think it's the most exciting thing. As one gets older one
gets into this—well, it's like a race, before you get to the
waterfall, when you feel the water slowly getting quicker and
quicker, and you can't get out, and all you want to do is
get to the waterfall and over the edge. How exciting it is!
Why do people grumble about age so much? Mind you, I
suppose if I was disabled, I mean if you really are terribly
ill—well, good heavens, take yourself away, take yourself off.
I've had so many people write letters to me after they read
poems of mine—nearly every poem's about suicide, more or
less—how can they do it? My poem 'Exeant' is about taking
one's own life and the right one has to do this, and one has
the power to summon God, because death is a god, and he
has to come when we call him. It's one thing you must decide
for yourself. One mustn't bore anyone with it.

But you wouldn't like to be dead, would you?

Yes, I think it must be marvellous. Well, it might be
something rather nice. I don't know. It's either something
or nothing. I just feel optimistic. I don't know why. What
pulls one up from these terrible depressions—it's the thought
that it's in your own hands, that you can if you want to,
make an end of it, but one never does. Some people do,
obviously, but I've been more fortunate. I'm supposed to be
an agnostic, but I'm sort of a backslider as a believer, too.
I mean I'm a backslider as a non-believer, because every now
and then I think, 'No, I have this feeling that . . .'—well, it
really comes in the Lord's Prayer, which of course is the most
wonderful thing that's ever been said at the end, and people
sort of gabble it off who don't really think what it means.
Then it suddenly strikes one what it does mean—that last
bit, 'Thine is the Kingdom, the Power and the Glory', it's
absolutely marvellous. It means that absolute good, absolute
good, is in control of everything. Therefore of course one
longs to die, because it would be more in control there than
here, because being alive is like being in enemy territory. I
think one feels that this ultimate good, God, has abdicated
his power in this world. There, you'll feel at home—that's
what Heaven is, and of course I have written a lot about
that too.

Therefore you don't mind getting old?

I really enjoy it because so many things fall away that mattered when one was earning one's living. And one had to go out, however tired one was. One had to turn up and do one's job. And now, if I'm very tired, I just stay in bed. I like being very tired, I enjoy being very tired. But this is a very selfish point of view. Some people's old age isn't happy at all if they continue to have worries about money, and they haven't any money at all, and they have to go into some terrible home where everybody's so cheerful—I mean it's death, isn't it? Did you see that poem I wrote, 'Scorpion', in the *Nation* the other week? Well, it expresses it really. You see, Scorpion's got a new grievance—he's a wonderful animal, and his new grievance is that his soul has not been required of him. So it starts off with this wonderful line, a quotation from the Bible, 'This Night Shall Thy Soul Be Required of Thee'. Scorpion: 'My soul is never required of me, it always has to be somebody else of course. Will my soul be required of me tonight, perhaps?' Then Scorpion: 'I often wonder what it would be like to have one's soul required of one, but all I can think of is the outpatient's department. "Are you Mrs Briggs dear?" "No, I'm Scorpion." ' Then it goes on, why he wants this: 'I like to think that my soul will be required of me so that I can waft over the green grass to the blue sea. It must be quite empty, I don't want anyone else to be there. Other people can find somewhere else to go.' Then it ends with these two lines: 'Oh Lord God, please come and require the soul of thy scorpion. Scorpion so wishes to be gone.' Oh isn't that wonderful! I do think it's beautiful—oh, beg pardon!

Did you nearly marry, as Pompey in Novel on Yellow Paper *nearly did?*

Oh no—well yes, I suppose I did really. At that period I thought it was the right thing to do, one ought to—that it was the natural thing to do, hey-ho—but I wasn't very keen on it. Then I felt I couldn't possibly manage it, I couldn't be good enough. I felt, 'If you're going to be a wife, you must be a good wife.' I didn't feel up to it, I didn't feel strong enough. I'm much too selfish really. I'm much more interested in what I'm thinking about, and I shouldn't recognize him in the street probably. And you might get very tired too, this feeling of tiredness I've had all my life—sort of trapped in it. Well, then you'd suddenly see someone you adored beginning to dislike you very much. You don't want your wife to be tired all the time; you want to go out and have fun and so on, and you'd get tireder and tireder, and then this love would turn to hatred, and I didn't wish to be exposed to such hazards. I'm very fond of children. Why I admire children so much is that I think all the time, 'Thank heaven they aren't mine.' I remember a middle-aged, very shy man who had never met a poet before. He looked at me hard across the dinner-table and at last he said, 'Writing a poem must be like having a child.' I said, 'Good heavens, it isn't; I don't have a poem on my hands for twenty years'. Come to that, you might have a child on your hands for much longer, and you might have the grandchildren too. I feel so many theories are made up about life. Sort of journalistic ones. Like Bernard Levin who said the other day that England had lost an Empire and hadn't found a role. It couldn't be less true, because the English are very unself-conscious about themselves. The Americans are self-conscious about the English. The English just want to be themselves and not to have to bother to think about other people very much. All they ask is not to have to think about Ireland. The Irish are such bores, they will sort of go on and on.

What do you think about your novels now?

I like *The Holiday* very much better than *Novel on Yellow Paper*. There are lots of things in *Novel On Yellow Paper* that I don't like, partly the manner. I don't quite know where that manner comes from. It was the first thing I ever wrote, and just before I started writing it, I remember a friend of mine lent me some of Dorothy Parker whom I hadn't read before, and I got this rhythm very much into my mind, this sort of pseudo (for me) American accent which I can't stand. It dates; it doesn't seem to me to come quite naturally. Well, *The Holiday*'s got none of that; it hasn't got those mannerisms, and also it's a period when I was older. It's just after the war. I wrote it actually during the war and I couldn't get it published—my word, nobody would take it. I kept on putting in things that were after the war, like the troubles in Palestine, and it was in such a muddle that I had to call it the after-the-war period. The chapter which is called Over Dew had been a short story, but I couldn't get it published. I think it's very beautiful. Well, not very long ago I was reading this thing, and I thought, 'This is not prose, it falls into verse,' and I said, 'If it doesn't fall into verse I'm going to help it'. So I copied it out again and sold it as a poem, 'The House of Over-Dew'. Then it was published in my American book, *The Best Beast*, which isn't published over here, because it's mostly the stuff that's published over here. I don't know whether to call it Overdew, which suggests it's rather a long time coming along, or Over-dew which suggests rising damp. I gave *The Holiday* to my present publisher, and he couldn't make head or tail of it. He said, 'This is a terribly difficult book to read, Stevie; I don't know what to make of it, but a lot of it, Stevie, is really poems, you know.'

What do you think of the world today?

Well, much the same as I always thought of it yesterday. It doesn't change very much does it? People are so conceited, dip themselves in self-abasement and so on, and about never having been through such terrible times. Why, the Catholic Church are always saying how villainous the cruelty of the Nazis, but after all the Nazis—though God knows they were hell—only lasted thirteen years. The Inquisition went on for seven hundred years. I never can understand why the Catholics are so modest about their performance in the field of persecution. They so easily come first. They can't face it, can they? Talk about their wonderful habit of suppression of the truth and suggestion of the false.

Poetry today?

I never read it. I'm too nervous. It's not arrogance, it's that I'm afraid of getting caught up in it. I'm no judge of it at all. I'm astonished the young like my poems. They're rather melancholy on the whole. When I say to them, 'I can't see what you see in them, because on the whole they're a bit deathwards in their wish . . .' and I should have thought that the attitude of the young was more courageous than mine—not that there's much difference between youth and age. That's another journalistic idea, because, the poor darlings—well, what is youth? It's immaturity. Another few

years they'll be old—it's an arithmetical statement. I can't
see what youth sees in my poetry. I'd like to know. I can
see my poems have a romantic appeal, but a lot of it is
deathwards. I did an anthology for children and when they
sold the book to America they left 'children' out of the title.
I can't remember all my poems. I've written about 1000.
I'll sing you 'Do Take Muriel Out'. (*Stevie sang.*) It's very
Germanic, that.

You said in Novel on Yellow Paper *that in order to understand Pompey one had to understand Racine's* Phèdre. *Would
you say that about yourself?*

No, I wouldn't, because it's rather immodest. It's a play
that means a lot to me. A play I would go to when I've been
depressed and terribly sad. I've always re-read *Phèdre,* and
I always find it so wonderful, but I don't see any relation
between the character of Phèdre and me. She's much simpler
than I am. She's in those tragic circumstances in which she's
forced by this wretched goddess. I mean the whole thing is
that Venus has this hatred of her family and leaves them no
peace at all. A character to be so much in another's power
has to be a simple character. I'm straightforward but I'm not
simple. I love this character of Phèdre probably because it's
so opposite to mine. It's truly romantic. She's forced into
this tragic situation. In some ways I'm romantic but my
basic root is profoundly sensible—profoundly sensible. About
everything. There is a balance; I am aware of a balance. I
can be knocked off my balance. I know the sort of things that
can knock me off my balance—snakes. If I'm very tired I'm
very easily knocked off by talking too much. If you're with
somebody who's terribly boring and you can't get away—I'm
off my balance by that. I could almost jump out of the window.
I so easily get to that point. This is very much one's state
of health, low state of health working against one's natural
commonsense. I have a natural commonsense. It doesn't
sound very poetic, but I think I have a natural commonsense.
The popular notion that a poet has straws in the hair—quite
untrue.

How do your poems come?

Well, like this interview, you want masses of material and
then you shape. With my poems I just nag on. For instance,

E

I wrote a poem which only had two verses and sent the two verses to Anthony Thwaite*, and when he wrote back asking for more, I'd already written four more verses. It's about my sister having a stroke. I'll just run through it.

I was a beautiful plant, I stood in the garden supreme,
Till there came a blight that fell on each leaf,
How I wish this had not been,
Oh how I wish this had not been.
I can feel the sun and my blighted leaves
In an elderly way grow glad,
But oh in my depths I bleed, I bleed,
From a heart that is youthful and sad,
A heart that is fiercer than sad.

Well, that's the end. I thought it was enough, and then I went on:

Oh, feeling of youth, you had better go,
You are trapped by my age and deceased too.
Goodbye, goodbye, I will send you away,
There is nothing here now to please you.
Then my feeling of youth said, 'No, I will not go;
I will comfort you with love and pain.
And also, if you like, I can procure for you a potion
That you will not take in vain.
The torpors of age could not seize the notion
To drink of the freeing grain, to measure the freeing grain.
All the same, I should not take it if I were you,
As you always can, but rather see life with me through.

Then the last verse is:

It is not very long compared with geological time,
It is heaven to think of geological time.
The weight lifts . . . and this gives you a happy mind . . .

I've only just finished writing these extra verses. I was going to call it 'Thoughts About the Stroke'.†
I want to ask you about love.
You've asked me about love.
Oh, I can ask again. When did I ask you about love?

*Literary Editor of the *New Statesman*.
†This poem has not yet been published.

Well, you asked me about getting married.

That's not necessarily love.

Oh, I think it is. Oh, I don't know. I can't remember. It's so long ago, isn't it? I don't feel happy in love. I think I'm much happier in sort of friendships, you know. Having someone you can giggle with and have fun. I mean men. I adore that. As soon as I get on to the other side—it's a bit odd somehow, but I get sort of frightened.

Tell me about your Queen's Gold Medal for Poetry?

It was last year. Of course I was very nervous. I thought 'I'm sure to be late, I'm always late.' So of course as a result I got there terribly early, when they were changing the guard. Crowds of people milling up against the rails, so I thought, 'Well, I've just got time to slip round to the gallery and get some picture postcards'. Which I did, and crammed my bag out with these picture postcards—a rather small bag. Then I went up to one of the police and he obviously didn't believe me, at least I thought he didn't. So I thought, 'I'd better go for another walk I suppose.' Then it came on to rain, and I suddenly got rather cross and thought, 'Well, I'm not going to walk round again.' So I just walked up, and said, 'Well, I'm supposed to be there, you know, an appointment with Her Majesty, to have this medal.' Then they did know about it, so I went in, and they were terribly nice. You go to the inner courtyard. I was met by rather a decorative young man in a naval uniform which was very nice, and he took me in, and then I sat in this outer room, whatever it's called, a huge room, alone with the lady-in-waiting who was a very agreeable gal and this young man, and we laughed and we had a very giggly time, because they'd obviously read it up a bit. They'd heard that I sang my poems as well, so they said could I sing one, so under my breath I hissed it at them. We had a very gay time. I adored that part of it. Well, then the one before me came out, a staggering-looking woman. Well, I thought, I'm not properly dressed for this. I looked at her. She was tremendously made-up. I thought, 'I don't think there was quite enough really. I think I ought to have something above the waist.' You curtsey when the door's flung open. The young man took me to the door, and far away—the room's as big as Trafalgar Square—standing against the mantelpiece was this charming figure—the Queen. You curtsey, and you make your way across the room. Then she comes forward and smiles—she's got a very gracious smile—and gives you the medal. And as she gave it to me she said, 'I don't know what you'll do with it,' and I looked at it and said, 'Well, I suppose I could have a hook put on it and wear it round my neck. It's very beautiful, isn't it?' 'Well,' she said, 'I don't know whether it's real', and I said, 'Beg your pardon'. 'Oh,' I said, 'I'm sure it is.' Then she motioned me—I think that's the expression—to sit down. There was a table between. They'd told me outside not to worry about when to come out because she'd ring a bell under the table. Well, the poor darling kept on asking me questions about poetry. I rather got the impression it wasn't her favourite subject. You feel you're with an enormously charming woman and a very professional Queen. I mean, the grip on things. She made me feel awfully like a schoolgirl again, being interviewed by a rather cordial headmistress, but knowing that headmistresses aren't always like that. Then we talked about poetry, and I got rather nervous and said, 'I don't know why, but I seem to have written rather a lot about murder lately', which was rather an unfortunate thing to say. I'd just written that very long one based on the moors murder case, so I started to tell her the story, and the smile got rather fixed. She is absolutely charming, a totally different sort of mind in the sense that it's not a poetical mind, but I mean on administration and grasp of politics and economics and all that, she's frightfully good, never a foot wrong. You can walk out backwards. When you get to the door you turn again and curtsey and come out, and then the young man and the girl get a taxi for you; and the taxi driver was very thrilled because he'd never been to the inner court before. I think it was entirely due to Day Lewis*, my getting the medal. He is very generous. He does read other people's poetry, unlike me.

Tell me a bit about the park I call Steviesmithland.

It's called Grovelands Park; it's at Southgate, which is part of Palmers Green district. When we first came here it was a private house. It belonged to a man called Captain Taylor

*Cecil Day Lewis, Poet Laureate.

and his family. I think the son was killed out riding. He fell on his head, or something awful happened like that. This was in the days when building was beginning, the suburb was beginning to grow up, so when the estate came on to the market, the council in those days had enough foresight to see that it would get very built up, so they bought it—very much to their credit. Then, I think about 1910, it was thrown open to the public. It is absolutely marvellous. They haven't altered it very much. It's still got a huge lake, which is the source of inspiration for a great many of my deep country poems about lakes and people getting bewitched, enchanted, *ensorcellé*. It's very beautiful, and often quite empty. It lies high and those huge oak trees are heavenly. You can see right over to the Hertfordshire hills. You can't really see any houses, which is what I like. We are very near the country here—six stations before you get to Hertford, and it's absolutely untouched open country, fortunately turned into Green Belt now. When I was walking through the woods the other day, I saw a huge dog-fox leap up from the bracken, twist in the air, and the sun catching its fur, and, as it turned, it was as red as the bracken, the bracken was as red as the fox. Then I came across a hunt, long after the fox had disappeared.

Thinking about Stevie

Reading through letters and postcards received from Stevie, to 'refresh my memory', a cliché she would have twisted into one of her delicious puns, made me feel at first that I could not write about her. The person in the correspondence comes through too vivid for actual description. Was there in my experience of Stevie some tangible object such as Proust's *madeleine* which, when dipped in tea, would release the vast resources of the memory and bring it all back? I think all her friends would feel as ill-equipped, indeed as near helpless, as I do to recreate her for the stranger's delight, for, in her, friendship was a gift like intelligence and imagination.

Hers was a nature born for friendship, always ready to give and receive it, delighting in the play of affection and understanding, instantly able to add other links without in any way weakening links already forged. In simple terms, she was a 'natural' in the realm of popular appeal, which accounts, I think, for the way she was liked immediately by people of both sexes and all age groups—this until the end.

In his moving radio obituary tribute, Anthony Thwaite stressed how great an idol Stevie was with the 'pop' poets, meaning her younger peers, and, indeed, this was one of the oustanding features of Stevie—her attraction, both personally and in her work, for the young. Generally, poets in her age group, even when respected and admired, do not escape criticism from what is journalistically termed 'generation-gap' censure. This is not to say that her poetry appealed exclusively to the young. Quite the contrary: as one grows older it acquires deeper layers of meaning—but I am in danger of straying into literary assessment which is not now my brief. What I am trying to say is that Stevie herself was so much her work, or rather that her work illustrates her grasp of the joy and absurdity of life, and simultaneously of its pain and brevity.

Stevie's melancholy, about which she was so conscious, is an intrinsic *'petite phrase'* in her work; a refusal for one

moment to regard death as anything but life's inevitable
shadow constituted for Stevie a positive sonata of gaiety. She
was permanently interested in life: she held out both hands
to everyone. She had an immense capacity for non-sexual love,
and radiated generosity of being; which is not to say that
she was not witty about the failings of others, but that her
wit lacked malice. Her instinct was to love, and I think that
her tenderness towards animals (so luminously expressed
in her drawings) was an expression of regret that human
beings, in spite of reason, were all too prone to savage one
another.

Although there was a disparity in our ages of about a
decade and a half, Stevie was my contemporary in the sense
that Ivy Compton-Burnett could never be. Ivy was a celebrity
when I first entered her world, but Stevie was part of my
world in a very practical sense. That is, we were both what
she would have called 'working girls' when we first met in
1943. This was in the building we entitled The Tower—that
large complex of George Newnes' publishing offices, just off
the Strand. I was Assistant Editor of *John O'London's Weekly*,
while Stevie, a resident of The Tower for many years,
secretaried 'as a faithful dog-o' to the two baronets, Sir
Neville Pearson and Sir Frank Newnes, coming to them
straight from Mrs Hoster's Secretarial Training College. A sort
of Stevie mythology had come into being among the Newnes
staff, which, if slightly apocryphal, had a dash of truth, that
Stevie's baronets employed plain-spun secretarial helpers to
type their letters because Stevie was far too busy writing her
own novels and poems. Certainly the title of her first novel
was due to the fact that she typed it during Newnes-hours
on the firm's yellow paper reserved for carbon copies.

By the time I arrived at The Tower, Stevie was, certainly
to my way of thinking, a terrific celebrity: she had published
two novels and two volumes of poetry, and I owned copies
of all four books. The news that the author of *Novel On Yellow
Paper* and *Tender Only To One* actually worked in The
Tower was immeasurably exciting. Her work had hit the
headlines when it first appeared; she was not merely fear-
fully fashionable, but revolutionary and daring to those
of us in our twenties at the beginning of the war. We had,

to my knowledge, two friends in common, George Orwell and George Stonier, and I wondered which to use by way of introduction. Stevie took the decision from me: she inspected me, as it were, by coming up from her first floor to my fifth, and looking through old files. The fact that she did not utter a word during her first three visits rather shook me. At about her fourth call she came over to my desk and said, 'George told me you worked here'. I never thought to enquire *which* George.

Stevie was everything I wished a writer and a poet to be, full of wonder and word wisdom. Her relationship with the baronets seemed to me even more fantastical than Tower gossip, as I listened to Stevie's anecdotes of her Newnes working life: how she trotted to Harrods to buy soap for one of the baronets' mother; how she attended spiritualist (or was it theosophical?) sessions with the other, who, when taking her to lunch, always insisted on patronizing the coffee stall near Trafalgar Square; and how one of them actually advised her to invest in corset shares: 'They're going up, Stevie, they're going up.'

Her own habitat in the office (a real pad this) on the first floor matched her marvellously: a small high windowless room, door always open (had it a door? now I incline to doubt it), walls decorated with a selection of Stevie's drawings where one would often find her stirring what looked like a jumbo-size umbrella-stand with a shooting-stick. This object contained all those miscellanous writings sent in by people who failed to specify which of Newnes' various publications they wished their contributions to be considered by: these were sent up to the literary Miss Smith, who dropped them into her container, and, when, after some months of anxiety and nail-biting, an author enquired about his manuscript, Stevie very kindly would 'fish about' for it. 'In time', she said, 'it'll come to the top.' I am certain manuscripts are not so treated in these more time-and-motion-conscious days.

A series of inter-office notes was exchanged almost daily between the first and fifth floors via the Newnes try service (a gormless teenager), and pretty libellous some of these notes were, especially when my original editor, the late John

Brophy (whom Stevie and I adored because of his incredible
kindness and encouragement: he actually let us review books)
left. 'We can't really blame him', Stevie said, 'He's got to
think of his career'. We exchanged work-in-progress notes,
that is, about progress of work outside our weekly wage-
earning Newnes work, and in this way I acquired a wonderful
familiarity with the trials and tribulations of what Ivy had
called that 'extra occupation', which Stevie and I viewed as
our only possible one.

We lunched together, varying our restaurants according to
our budget, from Rules when we had something special to
celebrate—a new poem of Stevie's accepted, or a first review
by me—the Arts Theatre Club, where we could just sit and
read the weeklies for free—this when funds were low—and if
pushed to it, a small Soho French restaurant where we got a
six-course lunch (one of the courses a dish of radishes) for
about 2s. 6d. If funds did not permit at all, and the weather
was not too sullen, we would sit in the inner courtyard of
Inigo Jones's Covent Garden Church, itself a secret city-
garden, where on a bench Stevie would try out new poems on
me, which is to say that she would read them to me. It was
in that garden that she once showed me a photograph of an
angry swan, and told me that it was Edith Sitwell, from
whom she⁻ had received it. We nattered shamelessly, and
with, I hope, some wit, about mutual friends battling their
way to fame in literary circles: 'If there's one thing I do love
it's a common friend', Stevie said.

My favourite story of that period concerns an occasion
when it was decided that I should pay (mostly we went
dutch), and somehow we disagreed about the restaurant,
so we lunched on opposite sides of the same Soho street and
Stevie sent her bill over to me. 'Ah, you've dined out a lot
on that one', Stevie said to me a year ago when I repeated it
in her presence.

Often she would come up to Hampstead and, because of
the air-raids, stay the night. On one such visit Stevie brought
with her a large circular biscuit-tin which had a reproduction
of the obnoxious 'Bubbles' painting on its lid. In this she kept
her drawings. She sat on the floor and picked them over,
saying every now and then, 'I think I'll write a poem to

that one' in much the same way as a composer might suggest setting to music a classical lyric.

She also brought into my life that fascinating writer Anna Sebastian, who died so tragically in her thirties. Friedl (her real name) and Stevie together were hilarious, like two slap-happy clowns: both had the same total lack of time sense and brought out the more ghoulish side of each other's humour.

Stevie enjoyed being a guest. She once gave a party in a friend's house and wrote on her invitation, 'I am so looking forward to it, *never* having been anything but a guest all my slothful life', which wasn't quite true because in her own Palmers Green house she entertained with immense pleasure. She particularly enjoyed country weekends, and although she would joke about being fussy in her choice of hosts (could she be sure of a hot-waterbottle and a glass of hot milk at bedtime?) she was easy to please, fitting naturally into anyone's routine, unfailingly prompt with her thank-you letters. She also had a nice way of dealing with one's own casualness: 'Your invitations, dear, remain peculiarly your own. One day I shall write in the same vein "Dear Kay, I am giving a party. Will you ring up and find out when?" '. Stevie in the country was, to some extent, rather different from the town Stevie, less restless, more relaxed. In the country she felt safer, more in tune, less menaced perhaps. She adored downlands and trees, long walks and the sea. Her letters glisten with happiness when she describes her favourite East Coast holidays. Postcards from her on such holidays were in the following vein: '*How's your bank balance?* Heavenly here, very rough seas, very rough bathing, but I love it. I feel in the most boisterous good health—and *quite unintellectual*. This is the life I really like, dear, and let Literature go hang.'

Physically Stevie changed very little over the years, that is, if one discounts the basic streak of ill-health which always caught up with her periodically, and reduced her activities. She was clearly very happy about her increasing fame. In her way, she had fought hard for this, in the sense that after leaving Newnes (failing health forced an early retirement), she had had to increase her income by reviewing and other literary journalism. Also, oddly enough, she had had a gap in her success-line. Having launched off as a dazzling new star with *Novel On Yellow Paper* and the first two books of poetry and the whole publicity roundabout which goes with early success, for quite a while, after the war, she actually had difficulty selling her poems: 'There's no two ways about it. The Mandarins do not like my poems and I am beginning to think they might be right and I had better concentrate on learning to cook.' Also she found it not easy to place her third novel, *The Holiday*: 'What shall I call it? Do you think *Death and the Girl?*'. She rather exaggerated the number of publishers who had rejected this book. She took all these setbacks splendidly, wittily retelling stories of rejections from various periodicals which later would clamour to publish any poem of hers. 'Not Waving but Drowning' represented a real experience: 'If you attempt to be more melancholy than me I shall be more than furious: I shall be *hurt*. I felt too low for words (eh?) last weekend, but worked it off for all that in a poem, and *Punch* like it, think it *funny* I suppose. It was touching, I thought—called "Not Waving But Drowning".'

I myself had the pleasure of publishing her poetry in *The Windmill** and invited her to write about L. P. Hartley's 'Eustace and Hilda' triology. 'I adore the chap', Stevie said. She also wrote a ghost story, 'Is there a Life Beyond the Gravy?' for an anthology of new strange stories which I edited. She greatly enjoyed reading translations of her poems and was 'awfully bucked' with both the French and Spanish versions by the editors of the BBC's French and Latin American services for scripts I had written about her work.

About *The Holiday* she wrote 'I think it is *beautiful*, never brassy like *Novel On Yellow Paper*, but so richly melancholy like those hot summer days when it is so full of that calm before the autumn, it quite ravishes me. When I read it, the tears stream down my face because of what Matthew Arnold says, you know:

> But oh, the labour
> O Prince, what pain.'

*A literary quarterly, published by Heinemann, which I edited under a pseudonym. There were thirteen issues, the first six edited jointly with Reginald Morre.

Stevie knew the sweat, as well as the cost, of living only too well, and when in the sixties she really came to the climax of her fame, she was neither proud nor arrogant. Some of us often half protested at the way this later Stevie would expect from us what we called her 'fetch and carry' attitude. For example, the last time she was in Brighton, in 1970, she rang, from her hostess's house, another friend, asking that friend to telephone a third friend to come and collect her and drive her to see some other friends at a nearby hotel—and taxis are plentiful and easy to obtain in Brighton. But about her work she was surprisingly modest, continually astonished that it was so popular. Having previously been told that her work was too English, she naturally relished her new-found popularity in the United States—with poems in the *New Yorker*, and her books published. She knew the worth of her work, but did not expect others to be quite as perceptive, although I am sure she would not have put it so brashly.

My last memories of Stevie is of her reading her poems at the opening of the 1970 Brighton Festival at an extraordinarily macabre exhibition, *Death, Heaven and the Victorians*. Stevie was in pain because she had just cracked three ribs and injured again the knee which, some years previously, had been operated on. The next day she asked me to join her and a few friends for a picnic lunch a few yards away from my seafront flat. It was a day filled with that special clarity of light which Brighton is famous for. Stevie spoke about the possibility of selling her Palmers Green house and coming to live in Brighton. 'I do so love this stretch of beach and that wonderful pier.' Often, now, I can almost imagine that I see Stevie, sitting there on that shingle with the tide coming in, waving at me, as she did that day when I went to join her picnic party.

Also available in paperback from Allison & Busby

MORE WOMEN THAN MEN
Ivy Compton-Burnett

"There is no book of Miss Compton-Burnett's that has not its violent shock, as trim and tidy as a hand-grenade and as destructive potentially." — Pamela Hansford Johnson

Josephine Napier, headmistress of a girls' school, is a woman whose mask of amiable authority disguises a ruthless ability to manipulate others. But past and present conspire to threaten her absolute control and the machinations that follow draw the reader into a claustrophobic world of personal and sexual relations revealed through dialogue of a razor-edged politeness and wit.

ELDERS AND BETTERS
Ivy Compton-Burnett

"It becomes possible to suggest a reason for the fascination these singular novels exercise on a body of readers. What essentially they offer, their peculiar virtue, is the repetition of one and the same human situation, an acting-out of powerful impulses that run counter to an accepted social morality — brutal truth-telling, repressed family hatreds and loves, including the impulse to subdue weaker and younger members." — Storm Jameson, *Spectator*

Elders and Betters is one of Ivy Compton-Burnett's most powerful and characteristic novels in which the elders of a large, well-to-do family are by no means the betters.

IVY WHEN YOUNG
The Early Life of Ivy Compton-Burnett 1884-1919
Hilary Spurling

The first thirty-five years of Ivy Compton-Burnett's life were extra-ordinary — often much stranger than the events of her own novels. In this brilliant and exemplary biography Hilary Spurling shows how Ivy Compton-Burnett used the experiences of this period in the nineteen novels she wrote during the next fifty years of her life.

"A story of extraordinary fascination and drama...Mrs Spurling has done a brilliant job" — Anthony Powell, *Daily Telegraph*

"A definitive work...precise and consummate scholarship" — C.P. Snow, *Financial Times*

"The excellent first volume of what promises to be one of the most distinguished biographies of our time...Mrs Spurling writes with a graceful assurance and acute penetration" — Lettice Cooper, *Sunday Telegraph*

"A model literary biography, thorough, serious and witty" — *Listener*

"A superb book. I think it's one of the best biographies I've read in many years" — Paul Bailey

"A splendid piece of work, totally engrossing, consistently enthralling" — Kay Dick

"An extraordinary biography of an extraordinary woman" — Geoffrey Grigson